Five Comic
One-Act Plays

DOVER · THRIFT · EDITIONS

Five Comic One-Act Plays

ANTON CHEKHOV

DOVER PUBLICATIONS, INC.
Mineola, New York

DOVER THRIFT EDITIONS

GENERAL EDITOR: PAUL NEGRI
EDITOR OF THIS VOLUME: KATHY CASEY

Bibliographical Note

This Dover edition, first published in 1999, is an unabridged republication of English translations, by Constance Garnett, of five plays by Anton Chekhov, from a standard edition. The introductory Note was prepared for this edition.

Library of Congress Cataloging-in-Publication Data

Chekhov, Anton Pavlovich, 1860–1904.
    [Plays. English. Selections]
    Five comic one-act plays / Anton Chekhov.
       p.   cm. — (Dover thrift editions)
    Contents: An unwilling martyr—The anniversary—The proposal—The bear—The wedding.
    ISBN 0-486-40887-6 (pbk.)
    1. Chekhov, Anton Pavlovich, 1860–1904—Translations into English. I. Title.
II. Series.
PG3456.A19   1999
891.72'3—dc21
                                             99-31504
                                              CIP

Manufactured in the United States of America
Dover Publications, Inc., 31 East 2nd Street, Mineola, N.Y. 11501

Note

Anton Chekhov, the third of five children, was born in 1860 in the provincial town of Taganrog in south Russia. His father, who had been born a serf, tried to support the family by running a grocery store, but had to declare bankruptcy in 1876. As a boy, Anton worked in his father's store. He attended a local school and then studied for ten years at the town high school without earning a reputation as a good student. His studies left him with a lifelong dislike of the Greek and Latin classics. During those years, he was known for improvising humorous theatricals and mimicking teachers.

In 1876 his father moved the rest of the family to Moscow in hopes of making a fresh start. Anton continued at school in Taganrog, living alone and supporting himself by tutoring younger boys. He graduated in 1879, joined his family in Moscow, and began medical studies, earning his M.D. degree in 1884. While a medical student, he was the main support of his mother and two younger siblings, as his father could obtain only low-paying employment. Chekhov became quite popular as a prolific writer of humorous sketches, which were published in several St. Petersburg journals and newspapers.

After earning his medical degree, Chekhov began writing short stories on tragic themes, but humor remained an underlying element in much of his work. He always insisted that his major dramas were comedies, not tragedies. Until 1888 he used a pen name, but by the time he wrote the one-act plays in this volume, he was writing under his own name. These five "comic" plays explore the sometimes literally maddening absurdities, affronts, and relentless frustrations of everyday social interaction.

Chekhov practiced medicine only sporadically, but during the severe famine of 1891–92 he aided peasants felled by illness. In 1897 he suffered a lung hemorrhage caused by tuberculosis. He died in 1904. His letters, published posthumously, did not support the opinion of many contemporaries that life had seemed dreary to him.

Contents

An Unwilling Martyr   1

The Anniversary   9

The Proposal   23

The Bear   37

The Wedding   51

AN UNWILLING MARTYR

(A HOLIDAY EPISODE)

A JEST IN ONE ACT

Characters in the Play

IVAN IVANITCH TOLKATCHOV (*father of a family*)
ALEXEY ALEXEYITCH MURASHKIN (*his friend*)

The action takes place in Petersburg, in MURASHKIN'S
flat.

MURASHKIN's *study. Upholstered furniture.* MURASHKIN *is sitting at the writing-table. Enter* TOLKATCHOV, *holding in his arms a glass globe for a lamp, a toy bicycle, three hat-boxes, a large parcel of clothes, a fish-basket containing bottles of beer, and many small parcels. He looks about him in a dazed way and sinks exhausted on the sofa.*

MURASHKIN.   Hullo, Ivan Ivanitch! Delighted to see you! Where do you hail from?

TOLKATCHOV [*breathing hard*].   My dear fellow . . . I have a favour to ask you. . . . I entreat you . . . lend me a revolver till to-morrow. Be a friend!

MURASHKIN.   What do you want with a revolver?

TOLKATCHOV.   I need one. . . . Oh, holy saints! . . . Give me some water. . . . Make haste, water! I need it. . . . I have to pass through a dark wood to-night and so . . . to be ready for anything. Lend it me, there's a good fellow!

MURASHKIN.   Oh, nonsense, Ivan Ivanitch! What the devil's this about a dark wood? You've got something in your mind, I suppose? I can see from your face you are up to no good! But what's the matter with you? Are you ill?

TOLKATCHOV.   Stop, let me get my breath. . . . Oh, holy saints! I am as tired as a dog. I have a sensation all over my head and body as though I'd been beaten like a beefsteak. I can bear no more. Be a friend, ask no questions, don't go into details . . . give me a revolver! I implore you!

MURASHKIN.   Come, come, Ivan Ivanitch! What weakness! You, the father of a family, a civil councillor! For shame!

TOLKATCHOV.   Me the father of a family! I'm a martyr! I'm a beast of burden, a nigger, a slave, a coward who keeps waiting for something instead of despatching himself to the other world! I am a rag, a blockhead, an idiot! What am I living for? What's the object of it? [*leaps up*]. Tell me, please, what is it I am living for? Why this endless succession of moral and physical miseries? I can understand being a martyr for an idea, yes! but to be a martyr for goodness knows what, for lamp-shades

3

and ladies' petticoats. No! I'd rather not, thanks! No, no, no! I've had enough of it! Enough!

MURASHKIN.　Don't talk so loud, the neighbours will hear!

TOLKATCHOV.　The neighbours may hear for all I care! If you won't give me a revolver, someone else will—anyway, I shan't be long among the living! That's settled!

MURASHKIN.　Stop, you have pulled off my button. Speak coolly. I still don't understand what's wrong with your life.

TOLKATCHOV.　What's wrong? You ask what's wrong? Certainly, I'll tell you! By all means. Perhaps if I have it out, it will make me feel better. . . . Let us sit down. Come, listen. . . . Oh, dear, I can't get my breath! . . . Take to-day, for example. Take it. As you know from ten o'clock in the morning till four o'clock in the afternoon, I have to stick in the office. Baking hot, stuffy, flies, hopeless muddle and confusion. The secretary has taken a holiday, Hrapov has gone off to get married, the small fry of the office have gone dotty over week-ends, love affairs and amateur theatricals. . . . They are all worn out, sleepy and exhausted so that you can get no sense out of them. . . . The secretary's duties are being carried on by an individual deaf in the left ear and in love; the people who come to the office seem to have lost their wits, they are always in a hurry and a fluster—ill-tempered, threatening—such a regular Bedlam that you want to scream for help. Confusion and muddle! And the work is hellish: the same thing over and over again, enquiries and references—all the same like the waves of the sea. Your eyes are ready to drop out of your head, you know. Give me some water. . . . You come out of the office shattered, torn to rags. . . . You ought to have your dinner and a good snooze—but no, you've to remember that it's the summer holidays; that is, that you are a slave, a wretched rag, a miserable lost creature, and must run like a chicken, carrying out commissions. There is a charming custom in our country retreat: if the summer visitor is going to town, not only his wife, but every wretched holiday-maker is privileged and entitled to burden him with masses of commissions. My spouse insists on my going to the dressmaker and giving her a good scolding, because she has made the bodice too full and the shoulders too narrow; Sonitchka's shoes must be changed; my sister-in-law wants twenty kopecks' worth of crimson silk to match a pattern and two and a half yards of tape. . . . But wait a minute, here I'll read it to you. [*Takes a note out of his pocket and reads it*] A globe for the lamp; one pound of ham sausage; five kopecks' worth of cloves and nutmeg; castor-oil for Misha; ten pounds of granulated sugar; fetch from home the copper stewpan and the mortar for pounding sugar; carbolic acid, insect powder, ten kopecks' worth of face powder; twenty bottles of beer; vinegar and a pair of corsets, size 82, for Mlle. Chanceau. . . . Ough! and fetch from home Misha's greatcoat and goloshes. Those are the orders from my wife and family. Now for the commissions from my dear friends and neighbours, damnation take them. The Vlassins are keeping Volodya's name-day to-morrow; he is to have a bicycle bought him; Madame Vihrin, the wife of the lieutenant-colonel, is in an interesting condition, and so I have to go every day to the mid-wife and beg her to come. And so on, and so on. I have five lists in my pocket, and my handkerchief is nothing but knots. And so, my dear fellow, in the time between the office and the train, one's tearing about the town like a dog with its tongue out—tearing about and cursing one's life. From the draper's to the chemist's, from the chemist's to the dressmaker's, from the dressmaker's to the pork butcher's, and then back to the chemist's again. In one place you trip up, in another you lose your money, in the third you forget to pay and they run after you and make a row, in the fourth you tread on a lady's skirt . . . pfoo! Such a form of exercise sends one dotty and makes one such a wreck that every bone aches all night afterwards, and one dreams of crocodiles. Well, your tasks have been performed and everything has been bought—now kindly tell me how is one to pack all this truck? How, for instance, are you going to pack a heavy copper pan and a mortar with a globe for the lamp, or carbolic with tea? How are you going to combine bottles of beer and a bicycle? It's a labour of Hercules, a problem, a riddle! You may rack your brains and do your utmost, but in the end you are sure to break or spill something, and at the station and in the railway carriage you will have to stand with your legs straddling and your arms out, propping up some package with your chin, all hung with fish baskets, card-board boxes, and such trumpery. And when the train starts the pas-sengers begin hustling your parcels out of the way, for your luggage is all over other people's seats. They make a fuss, call the guard, threaten to have you turned out, but what am I to do? I simply stand and blink at them like a donkey when it is beaten. Now let me tell you what comes next. I get home to my summer villa. Then one does deserve a good drink after one's day of toil, a meal—a good snooze— doesn't one?—but not a bit of it! My wife keeps a sharp eye on me. You've scarcely swallowed your soup before she pounces on you and you must go, if you please, to private theatricals or a dancing club. Don't dare to protest. You are a husband, and the word "husband," translated into holiday language, means a dumb animal who can be driven and laden as you please, with no risk of interference from the Society for the Prevention of Cruelty to Animals. You go and stare at "A Scandal in a Respectable Family" or at "Motya"; you clap your hands at your wife's prompting while you grow weaker, and weaker, and weaker, and feel every minute as though you will expire. And at the club you have to look on at the dancing and find partners for your better-half, and if there are not gentlemen enough, you have to dance the quadrille yourself. You get home from the theatricals or the dancing after midnight, feeling more like a dead sheep than a human being. But now, at last, you reach the longed-for end; you have undressed and get into bed. Excellent, you can shut your eyes and go to sleep. . . . It's all so nice, so poetical, so snug, you know; the children are not screaming in the next room, and your wife is not there, and your conscience is at ease—you could wish for nothing better. You drop asleep—and all at once . . . all at once you hear, dz-z-z-z! The gnats! [*leaps up*]. The gnats, double damnation to them! [*shakes his fists*]. Gnats! They beat the plagues of Egypt, the tortures of the Inquisition! Dz-z-z! It buzzes so plaintively, so mournfully, as though it were asking your forgiveness; but it bites you, the rascal, so that you are scratching for an hour after. You smoke, you slaughter them, you cover up your head—there is no escape! In the end you curse and give yourself up to be devoured: let the damned brutes bite away! No sooner are you resigned to the gnats than another plague is upon you: your spouse begins practising songs with her tenors in the drawing-room. They sleep all day and spend the night getting up amateur concerts. Oh, my God! Those tenors are a torture, the gnats aren't in it! [*Sings*] "Tell me not thy youth is ruined" . . . "Spellbound again I stand before thee." . . . Oh, the be-easts! They wring the very soul out of my body! To deaden the sound of them a little I have to practise this trick: I tap myself with my finger just by my ear. I go on tapping like that till they go away at four o'clock. Och! Another drink of water, my boy. . . . I can't bear it. . . . Well, so after a night without sleep you get up at six o'clock and—off to the station for your train! You run, you are afraid of being late, and the mud! the fog! the cold—brr! When you get to town, it is the same old hurdy-gurdy over again! There it is! It's a beastly life, I tell you. I wouldn't wish my worst enemy such a life. It has made me ill, do you understand? Asthma, heartburn, I am always in a panic about something; my stomach won't work, my eyes are dizzy. . . . Would you believe it, I have become a regular neurotic . . . [*looks about him*]. Only this is strictly between ourselves. I should like to consult Tchetchott or Merzheyovsky. A sort of frenzy comes over me, my boy. When I am annoyed or driven silly, when the gnats bite or the tenors sing, I have a sudden dizziness before my eyes. I leap up and run all over the house as though I were crazy, shouting, "I thirst for blood! Blood!" And at such moments I really long to stick a knife into somebody or bash his head in with a chair. You see what this holiday life may bring one to! And no one is sorry for me, no one feels for me — they all take it for granted. They actually laugh. But can't you understand, I am a living creature, I want to live! This isn't a farce, it is a tragedy! If you won't give me a revolver, you might at least feel for me!

MURASHKIN.   I do feel for you.

TOLKATCHOV.   I see how you feel for me. . . . Good-bye, I must go and get anchovies, sausage . . . there's still the tooth-powder to get, too, and then to the station.

MURASHKIN.   Where are you staying for the holidays?

TOLKATCHOV.   At the Putrid River.

MURASHKIN [gleefully].   Really? I say, do you happen to know Olga Pavlovna Finberg who is staying there?

TOLKATCHOV.   I know her. She is a friend of ours, in fact.

MURASHKIN.   You don't say so! What luck! How fortunate! It would be nice of you . . .

TOLKATCHOV.   What is it?

MURASHKIN.   My dear friend, would it be possible for you to do me a small favour? Be a friend! Promise me you will do it?

TOLKATCHOV.   What is it?

MURASHKIN.   As a friend, I ask you! I entreat you, my dear boy. In the first place give my greetings to Olga Pavlovna, tell her that I am alive and well and that I kiss her hand. And in the second, take her something for me. She commissioned me to buy her a hand sewing-machine, and there is nobody to take it her. . . . Take it, my dear fellow! And while you are about it, you might as well take this cage with the canary . . . only do be careful, or the little door will get broken. . . . Why do you look at me like that?

TOLKATCHOV.   A sewing-machine . . . a bird-cage and canary . . . greenfinches . . . linnets . . .

MURASHKIN.   Ivan Ivanitch, what is the matter with you? Why are you so red in the face?

TOLKATCHOV [stamping].   Give me the sewing-machine! Where is the bird-cage? Get on my back yourself! Tear a man to pieces! Eat him up! Make an end of him! [clenches his fists]. I thirst for blood! for blood! for blood!

MURASHKIN.   You are mad!

TOLKATCHOV [*bearing down upon him*].   I thirst for blood! for blood!

MURASHKIN [*in terror*].   He's gone out of his mind! [*Shouts*] Petrusha! Marya! Where are you? Save me!

TOLKATCHOV [*chasing him about the room*].   I thirst for blood! For blood!

CURTAIN.

THE ANNIVERSARY

Characters in the Play

ANDREY ANDREYEVITCH SHIPUTCHIN (*Chairman of the Board of Management of the N— Mutual Credit Bank, a youngish man with an eyeglass*)
TATYANA ALEXEYEVNA (*his wife, age 25*)
KUZMA NIKOLAYEVITCH HIRIN (*the Bank Cashier, an old man*)
NASTASYA FYODOROVNA MERTCHUTKIN (*an old woman in a pelisse*)
Members of the Board of Management
Bank Clerks

The action takes place in the N— Mutual Credit Bank.

The chairman's office. On the left a door leading to the counting-house. Two writing-tables. The office is furnished with pretensions to refined taste: velvet upholstery, flowers, statues, rugs. Telephone. Midday.
HIRIN *alone; he is wearing felt overboots.*

HIRIN [*shouts at the door*].   Send someone to the chemist's for three pennyworth of valerian drops and tell them to bring some clean water to the chairman's office! Am I to tell you a hundred times? [*Goes to the table.*] I am utterly worn out. I have been writing for the last three days and nights without closing my eyes; from morning till night I am at work here, and from night till morning at home [*coughs*]. And I feel ill all over! Shivering, feverish, coughing, my legs ache and there are all sorts of . . . stops and dashes before my eyes [*sits down*]. That affected ass, our scamp of a chairman, will read a report to-day at the general meeting: "Our bank at present and in the future." A regular Gambetta . . . [*writes*]. Two . . . one . . . one . . . six . . . nought . . . six. . . . He wants to cut a dash and so I have to sit here and work for him like a galley-slave! . . . He has put in nothing but the lyrical touches in the report and has left me to work for days together adding up figures, the devil flay his soul . . . [*counts on reckoning frame*]. I can't endure the man [*writes*]. One . . . three . . . seven . . . two . . . one . . . nought. . . . He promised to reward me for my work. If everything goes off well to-day and he succeeds in hoodwinking the public, he promised me a gold medal and a bonus of three hundred. . . . We shall see [*writes*]. But if I get nothing for my trouble you must look out for yourself. . . . I am a hasty man. . . . I may do anything if I am worked up. . . . Yes!

[*Behind the scenes there is a noise of applause. Voice of* SHIPUTCHIN: "Thank you, thank you! I am touched!" *Enter* SHIPUTCHIN. *He is wearing a dress-coat and white tie; in his hands an album which has just been presented to him.*]

SHIPUTCHIN [*standing in the doorway and looking towards the*

11

counting-house]. I shall keep this present of yours, dear colleagues, to the day of my death in memory of the happiest days of my life! Yes, gentlemen! I thank you once more [*waves a 'kiss and walks up to* HIRIN]. My dear, good Kuzma Nikolayevitch!

[*While he is on the stage* Clerks *come in occasionally with papers for him to sign, and go out again.*]

HIRIN [*getting up*]. I have the honour to congratulate you, Andrey Andreyevitch, on the fifteenth anniversary of our bank, and hope that . . .

. SHIPUTCHIN [*presses his hand warmly*]. Thank you, dear old man, thank you! In honour of this glorious occasion, in honour of the anniversary, I think we might even kiss each other. [*They kiss.*] I am very glad, very. Thanks for your good work, for everything! If I've done anything useful during my period of office as chairman of the Board of Management, I am indebted for it above all to my colleagues [*sighs*]. Yes, old man, fifteen years, fifteen years as sure as my name's Shiputchin! [*Eagerly*] Well, what about my report? Is it getting on?

HIRIN. Yes. There are only five pages left.

SHIPUTCHIN. Good. Then by three o'clock it will be ready?

HIRIN. If nobody hinders me, I shall get it done. There's very little left to do.

SHIPUTCHIN. Splendid. Splendid, as sure as my name's Shiputchin! The general meeting will be at four o'clock. I say, my dear fellow, let me have the first half, I'll go over it. . . . Make haste, give it me [*takes the report*]. . . . I expect great things from this report. . . . It's my *profession de foi*, or rather my fireworks . . . fireworks, as sure as my name's Shiputchin! [*sits down and reads the report*]. I am devilish tired, though. . . . I had an attack of gout in the night, I spent all the morning racing about doing things, and then this excitement, this ovation . . . so upsetting! I am tired!

HIRIN [*writes*]. Two . . . nought . . . nought . . . three . . . nine . . . two . . . nought. . . . The figures make my eyes dizzy. . . . Three . . . one . . . six . . . four . . . one . . . five . . . [*rattles the reckoning beads*].

SHIPUTCHIN. Another unpleasantness. . . . Your wife came to me this morning and complained of you again. She said that you ran after her and your sister-in-law with a knife yesterday. Kuzma Nikolayevitch, what next! Aie, aie!

HIRIN [*sourly*]. I will venture, Andrey Andreyevitch, in honour of the anniversary, to ask a favour of you, and beg you, if only out of consideration for my working like a slave, not to meddle in my family affairs! I beg you!

SHIPUTCHIN [*sighs*]. You have an impossible temper, Kuzma

Nikolayevitch! You are an excellent, estimable person, but with women you behave like some Jack the Ripper! You really do. I can't understand why you hate them so.

HIRIN.   And I can't understand why you like them so! [*A pause.*]

SHIPUTCHIN.   The clerks have just presented me with an album and the members of the Board, so I hear, are going to present me with an address and a silver tankard . . . [*playing with his eyeglass*]. It's fine, as sure as my name's Shiputchin! . . . It's all to the good. . . . We must have a bit of splash for the sake of the bank, deuce take it! You are one of ourselves, you know all about it, of course. . . . I composed the address myself, I bought the silver tankard myself too. . . . And there, the binding of the address cost 45 roubles. But we have to have that. They would never have thought of it themselves [*looks round him*]. Just look at the get-up of the place! Isn't it fine? Here they tell me that it is petty of me to want the locks on the doors to be polished and the clerks to wear fashionable ties, and to have a stout porter at the entrance. Not a bit of it, my good sir! The locks on the doors and the stout porter are not a petty matter. At home I may be a vulgarian, I may eat and sleep like a pig and drink till I am crazy. . . .

HIRIN.   No insinuations, please!

SHIPUTCHIN.   Nobody is making insinuations! What an impossible temper you have. . . . Well, as I was saying, at home I may be a vulgarian, a parvenu, and give way to my habits, but here everything must be *en grand*. This is the bank! Here every detail must be impressive, so to speak, and have an imposing air! [*Picks up a scrap of paper from the floor and throws it into the fire.*] What I do take credit for is having raised the reputation of the bank. . . . Tone is a great thing! It's a great thing as sure as my name's Shiputchin. [*Scrutinising* HIRIN] My dear fellow, the deputation from the shareholders may be here any minute and you are in your felt overboots and that scarf . . . and a reefer jacket of some nondescript colour. . . . You might have put on a dress-coat or a black frock-coat, anyway. . . .

HIRIN.   My health is more precious to me than your shareholders. I am suffering from inflammation all over.

SHIPUTCHIN [*growing excited*].   But you must own it's unsuitable? You spoil the *ensemble!*

HIRIN.   If the deputation comes in I can keep out of sight. It's no great matter . . . [*writes*]. Seven . . . one . . . seven . . . two . . . one . . . five . . . nought. I don't like anything unsuitable myself. Seven . . . two . . . nine . . . [*rattles the reckoning beads*]. I can't stand anything unsuitable. For instance, you would have done better not to have invited ladies to the anniversary dinner to-day!

SHIPUTCHIN.   What nonsense!

HIRIN.   I know you will let in a whole drawing-room full of them to make a fine show, only mind they'll spoil it all for you. They are the source of every trouble and mischief.

SHIPUTCHIN.   Quite the opposite. Feminine society has an elevating influence!

HIRIN.   Yes. . . . Your wife is highly cultured, I believe, but last Monday she said something so appalling that I couldn't get over it for two days after. All of a sudden, before outsiders, she blurted out: "Is it true that my husband has bought the Dryazhko-Pryazhky shares which have fallen on the exchange? Oh, my husband is so worried about them!" To say that before outsiders! And what you want to be so open with them for, I can't understand! Do you want them to get you into trouble?

SHIPUTCHIN.   Come, that's enough, that's enough! This is all too gloomy for an anniversary. By the way, you remind me [*looks at his watch*]. My better-half ought to be here directly. By rights I ought to have gone to the station to meet her, poor thing, but I haven't time and I'm . . . tired. To tell the truth I am not glad she is coming. That is, I am glad, but it would have been pleasanter for me if she had stayed another two days at her mother's. She will expect me to spend the whole evening with her, and meanwhile we have planned a little excursion when the dinner is over . . . [*shivers*]. There, I am in a nervous shiver already. My nerves are so over-strained that I could burst into tears at the slightest provocation! No, I must be firm, as sure as my name's Shiputchin!

[*Enter* TATYANA ALEXEYEVNA *wearing a waterproof and with a travelling satchel slung across one shoulder.*]

SHIPUTCHIN.   Bah! Talk about angels!

TATYANA ALEXEYEVNA.   Darling! [*Runs to her husband; prolonged kiss.*]

SHIPUTCHIN.   And we were just talking about you!

TATYANA ALEXEYEVNA [*breathlessly*].   Have you missed me? Are you quite well? I haven't been home yet, I've come straight here from the station. I've got ever so much to tell you, ever so much. I can't wait . . . I won't take off my things, I've only looked in for a minute. [*To* HIRIN] How are you, Kuzma Nikolayevitch? [*To her husband*] Is everything all right at home?

SHIPUTCHIN.   Quite. Why, you've grown plumper and prettier in the week. Well, what sort of journey did you have?

TATYANA ALEXEYEVNA.   Splendid! Mamma and Katya send you their love. Vassily Andreyevitch asked me to give you a kiss from him [*kisses him*]. Aunt sends you a jar of jam and they are all angry with you

for not writing. Zina told me to give you a kiss from her [*kisses him*].
Ah, if only you knew what happened! What happened! I am positively
afraid to tell you! Oh, such a dreadful thing happened! But I see from
your face you're not glad to see me.

SHIPUTCHIN. Quite the contrary . . . darling . . . [*kisses her*].

[HIRIN *coughs angrily*.]

TATYANA ALEXEYEVNA [*sighs*].   Ah, poor Katya, poor Katya! I am so
sorry for her, so frightfully sorry!

SHIPUTCHIN.   It's our anniversary to-day, darling. The deputation
from the shareholders may turn up here any minute and you are not
dressed.

TATYANA ALEXEYEVNA.   Really? The anniversary? I congratulate
you, gentlemen. . . . I wish you . . . So there will be a party here to-day,
a dinner? I like that. . . . And do you remember that splendid address
you were so long making up for the shareholders? Will they read it to
you to-day?

[HIRIN *coughs angrily*.]

SHIPUTCHIN [*in confusion*].   We don't talk about that, darling. . . .
Really, you had better go home.

TATYANA ALEXEYEVNA.   In a minute, in a minute . . . I'll tell you all
about it in one instant and then go. I'll tell you all about it from the
very beginning. Well . . . when you saw me off I sat down, do you remember, beside that stout lady and began reading? I don't like talking
in the train. I went on reading for three stations and did not say a word
to anyone. . . . Well, evening came on and I began to have such de-
pressing thoughts, you know! There was a young man sitting opposite
who was quite all right, not bad-looking, rather dark. . . . Well, we got
into conversation. . . . A naval officer came up, then a student . . .
[*laughs*]. I told them I wasn't married. . . . How they flirted with me!
We talked till midnight. The dark young man told some awfully funny
stories and the naval officer kept singing. . . . My chest simply ached
with laughing. And when the officer—ah, those naval men!—when the
officer found out accidentally that my name was Tatyana, do you know
what he sang? [*Sings in a bass voice*] "Onyegin, I will not disguise it, I
love Tatyana madly!" . . . [*laughs*].

[HIRIN *coughs angrily*.]

SHIPUTCHIN.   But, Tanyusha, we are hindering Kuzma
Nikolayevitch. Go home, darling. Tell me later. . . .

TATYANA ALEXEYEVNA.   Never mind, never mind, let him listen, it's
interesting. I shall have finished directly. Seryozha came to the station

to fetch me. A young man turned up too, a tax inspector I believe he
was . . . quite all right, very nice, particularly his eyes. . . . Seryozha in-
troduced him and he drove back with us. It was glorious weather. . . .

[*Voices behind the scenes:* "You can't, you can't! What do you
want?" *Enter* MADAME MERTCHUTKIN.]

MADAME MERTCHUTKIN [*in the doorway, waving the clerks off*].
What are you holding me for? What next! I want to see the manager!
. . . [*Comes in to* SHIPUTCHIN] . . . I have the honour, your Excellency
. . . my name is Nastasya Fyodorovna Mertchutkin, wife of a provincial
secretary.

SHIPUTCHIN.   What can I do for you?

MADAME MERTCHUTKIN.   You see, your Excellency, my husband,
the provincial secretary Mertchutkin, has been ill for five months, and
while he was laid up at home in the doctor's hands he was discharged
from the service for no sort of reason, your Excellency. And when I
went for his salary, they deducted, if you please, your Excellency, 24
roubles 36 kopecks from it. "What's that for?" I asked. "Well," they told
me, "he borrowed that from the Mutual Benefit club and the other
clerks stood security for him." How is that? How could he borrow it
without my consent? That's not the way to do things, your Excellency!
I am a poor woman, I earn my bread by taking in lodgers. . . . I am a
weak, defenceless woman. . . . I have to put up with ill-usage from
everyone and never hear a kind word.

SHIPUTCHIN.   Excuse me [*takes her petition from her and reads it
standing*].

TATYANA ALEXEYEVNA [*to* HIRIN].   But I must tell you from the beginning. . . . Last week I suddenly got a letter from mamma. She wrote
to me that a certain Mr. Grendilevsky had made my sister Katya an
offer. An excellent, modest young man, but with no means and no def-
inite position. And unluckily, only fancy, Katya was very much taken
with him. What was to be done? Mamma wrote that I was to come at
once and use my influence with Katya.

HIRIN [*surlily*].   Excuse me, you put me out! You go on about
mamma and Katya and I've lost count and don't know what I am doing.

TATYANA ALEXEYEVNA.   As though that mattered! You ought to listen when a lady talks to you! Why are you so cross to-day? Are you in
love? [*laughs.*]

SHIPUTCHIN [*to* MADAME MERTCHUTKIN].   Excuse me, what's this?
I can make nothing of it.

TATYANA ALEXEYEVNA.   You're in love! A-ha! he is blushing!

SHIPUTCHIN [*to his wife*].   Tanyusha, go into the counting-house for
a minute, darling. I shan't be long.

TATYANA ALEXEYEVNA. Very well [*goes out*].

SHIPUTCHIN. I can make nothing of it. Evidently you have come to the wrong place, madam. Your petition has nothing to do with us at all. You will have to apply to the department in which your husband was employed.

MADAME MERTCHUTKIN. Why, my dear sir, I have been to five places already and they would not even take the petition anywhere. I'd quite lost my head, but my son-in-law, Boris Matveyitch—God bless him for it—advised me to come to you. "You go to Mr. Shiputchin, mamma," he said, "he is an influential man, he can do anything for you." . . . Help me, your Excellency!

SHIPUTCHIN. We can do nothing for you, Madame Mertchutkin. You must understand: your husband, so far as I can see, served in the Army Medical Department, and our establishment is a purely private commercial undertaking, a bank. Surely you must understand that!

MADAME MERTCHUTKIN. Your Excellency, I have the doctor's certificate that my husband was ill! Here it is, if you will kindly look at it!

SHIPUTCHIN [*irritably*]. Very good, I believe you, but I repeat it has nothing to do with us.

[*Behind the scenes* TATYANA ALEXEYEVNA's *laugh; then a masculine laugh.*]

SHIPUTCHIN [*glancing towards the door*]. She is hindering the clerks there. [*To* MADAME MERTCHUTKIN] It's queer and absurd, indeed. Surely your husband must know where you ought to apply.

MADAME MERTCHUTKIN. He knows nothing, your Excellency. He keeps on "It's not your business, go away"—that's all I can get out of him.

SHIPUTCHIN. I repeat, madam: your husband was in the Army Medical Department, and this is a bank, a purely private commercial undertaking.

MADAME MERTCHUTKIN. Yes, yes, yes. . . . I understand, sir. In that case, your Excellency, tell them to pay me fifteen roubles at least! I agree to take part on account.

SHIPUTCHIN [*sighs*]. Ough!

HIRIN. Andrey Andreyitch, at this rate I shall never have the report done!

SHIPUTCHIN. One minute. [*To* MADAME MERTCHUTKIN] There's no making you see reason. Do understand that to apply to us with such a petition is as strange as to send a petition for divorce to a chemist's, for instance, or to the Assaying Board.

[*A knock at the door,* TATYANA ALEXEYEVNA's *voice:* "Andrey, may I come in?"]

SHIPUTCHIN [*shouts*].   Wait a little, darling; in a minute! [*To* MADAME MERTCHUTKIN] You have not been paid your due, but what have we to do with it? Besides, madam, it's our anniversary to-day; we are busy . . . and someone may come in here at any minute. . . . Excuse me.

MADAME MERTCHUTKIN.   Your Excellency, have pity on a lone lorn woman! I am a weak, defenceless woman. . . . I am worried to death. . . . I have a lawsuit with my lodgers, and I have to see to my husband's affairs and fly round looking after the house, and my son-in-law is out of a job.

SHIPUTCHIN.   Madame Mertchutkin, I . . . No, excuse me, I cannot talk to you! My head is going round. . . . You are hindering us and wasting time . . . [*sighs, aside*]. She's an idiot, as sure as my name is Shiputchin! [*To* HIRIN] Kuzma Nikolayevitch, please will you explain to Madame Mertchutkin . . . [*with a wave of his hand goes out of the office*].

HIRIN [*going up to* MADAME MERTCHUTKIN, *surlily*].   What can I do for you?

MADAME MERTCHUTKIN.   I am a weak, defenceless woman. . . . I look strong perhaps, but if you were to overhaul me there isn't one healthy fibre in me! I can scarcely keep on my feet, and my appetite is gone. I drank my cup of coffee this morning without the slightest relish.

HIRIN.   I am asking you what I can do for you.

MADAME MERTCHUTKIN.   Bid them pay me fifteen roubles, sir, and I'll take the rest in a month's time.

HIRIN.   But you've been told already in plain words: this is a bank.

MADAME MERTCHUTKIN.   Yes, yes. . . . And if necessary I can produce a medical certificate.

HIRIN.   Have you got a head on your shoulders, or what?

MADAME MERTCHUTKIN.   My dear man, I am asking for what is my due. I don't want other people's money.

HIRIN.   I ask you, madam, have you got a head on your shoulders, or what? I'll be damned if I waste my time talking to you. I am busy. [*Points to the door*] Kindly walk out!

MADAME MERTCHUTKIN [*surprised*].   And what about the money?

HIRIN.   The fact is, what you've got on your shoulders is not a head, but this . . . [*taps with his finger on the table and then on his own forehead*].

MADAME MERTCHUTKIN [*offended*].   What? Come, come! . . . Talk to your own wife like that. . . . My husband is a provincial secretary! You'd better look out!

HIRIN [*firing up, in a low voice*].   Clear out!

MADAME MERTCHUTKIN.   Come, come, come! . . . Look out!

HIRIN [*in a low voice*].   If you don't leave the room this very minute, I'll send for the porter. Clear out! [*Stamps.*]

MADAME MERTCHUTKIN.   Not a bit of it! I am not afraid of you. I've seen the likes of you. . . . You screw!

HIRIN.   I don't believe I've ever in my life seen a nastier woman. . . . Ough! It makes me feel dizzy . . . [*breathing hard*]. I tell you once more . . . do you hear? If you don't leave the room, you old scarecrow! I'll pound you to a jelly. I've such a temper, I might cripple you for life! I might commit a crime!

MADAME MERTCHUTKIN.   More bark than bite. I'm not afraid of you. I've seen the likes of you.

HIRIN [*in despair*].   I can't bear the sight of her! I feel ill! I can't stand it [*goes to the table and sits down*]. They let loose a swarm of women on the bank: I can't write the report! I can't do it!

MADAME MERTCHUTKIN.   I am not asking for other people's money: I am asking for my own—for what is my lawful due. Ah, the shameless fellow! He is sitting in a public office with his overboots on. . . . The lout!

[*Enter* SHIPUTCHIN *and* TATYANA ALEXEYEVNA.]

TATYANA ALEXEYEVNA [*following her husband in*].   We went to an evening party at the Berezhnitskys'. Katya was wearing a pale blue foulard with light lace and a low neck. . . . It does suit her doing her hair up high, and I did it for her myself. . . . When she was dressed and had her hair done she looked simply fascinating!

SHIPUTCHIN [*by now suffering from migraine*].   Yes, yes . . . fascinating! . . . They may come in here in a minute.

MADAME MERTCHUTKIN.   Your Excellency!

SHIPUTCHIN [*despondently*].   What now? What can I do for you?

MADAME MERTCHUTKIN.   Your Excellency! [*Pointing to* HIRIN] Here, this man . . . he here, this man, tapped himself on the forehead and then tapped the table. . . . You told him to go into my case, and he is jeering at me and saying all sorts of things. I am a weak, defenceless woman.

SHIPUTCHIN.   Very good, madam; I will go into it. . . . I will take steps. . . . Go away! Later. [*Aside*] My gout is coming on!

HIRIN [*goes quietly up to* SHIPUTCHIN].   Andrey Andreyitch, send for the porter; let him kick her out! It's too much of a good thing!

SHIPUTCHIN [*in alarm*]. No, no! She'll set up a squeal, and there are lots of flats in the building.

MADAME MERTCHUTKIN. Your Excellency!

HIRIN [*in a tearful voice*]. But I've got to finish the report! I shan't finish it in time! . . . [*goes back to the table*]. I can't do it!

MADAME MERTCHUTKIN. Your Excellency, when shall I receive the money? I need it to-day.

SHIPUTCHIN [*aside, with indignation*]. A re-mar-kab-ly nasty woman. [*To her, softly*] Madam, I have told you already, this is a bank—a private commercial establishment.

MADAME MERTCHUTKIN. Do me a kindness, your Excellency! Be a father to me! . . . If the medical certificate is not enough, I can produce an affidavit from the police. Tell them to give me the money!

SHIPUTCHIN [*sighs heavily*]. Ough!

TATYANA ALEXEYEVNA [*to* MADAME MERTCHUTKIN]. Granny, you've been told that you are hindering them. It's too bad of you, really.

MADAME MERTCHUTKIN. My pretty lady, I've no one to take my part. I might just as well not eat or drink. I drank my cup of coffee this morning without the slightest relish.

SHIPUTCHIN [*exhausted, to* MADAME MERTCHUTKIN]. How much do you want?

MADAME MERTCHUTKIN. Twenty-four roubles thirty-six kopecks.

SHIPUTCHIN. Very good [*takes a twenty-five rouble note out of his pocket-book and gives it to her*]. Here is twenty-five roubles. Take it . . . and go!

[HIRIN *coughs angrily.*]

MADAME MERTCHUTKIN. Thank you kindly, your Excellency [*puts the money away*].

TATYANA ALEXEYEVNA [*sitting down by her husband*]. It's time for me to go home [*looking at her watch*]. . . . But I haven't finished my story. It won't take me a minute to tell you the rest, and then I am going. . . . Something so dreadful happened! And so we went to an evening party at the Berezhnitskys'. . . . It was all right—very jolly—but nothing special. . . . Of course, Katya's admirer Grendilevsky was there too. . . . Well, I had talked to Katya, I had cried; I'd used my influence; she had it out with Grendilevsky on that very evening and refused him. Well, I thought, everything is settled for the best: I had set mamma's mind at rest, I had saved Katya, and now I could be comfortable myself. . . . And what do you think? Just before supper Katya and I were walking along an avenue in the garden. . . . All of a sudden . . . [*excited*] all of a sudden we hear a shot. . . . No, I can't talk of it! [*Fans herself with her handkerchief.*] No, I can't!

SHIPUTCHIN [*sighs*].   Ough!

TATYANA ALEXEYEVNA [*weeping*].   We ran into the arbour, and there
. . . there lay poor Grendilevsky . . . with a pistol in his hand. . . .

SHIPUTCHIN.   No, I can't stand it! I can't stand it! [*To* MADAME
MERTCHUTKIN] What more do you want?

MADAME MERTCHUTKIN.   Your Excellency, couldn't you find another job for my husband?

TATYANA ALEXEYEVNA [*weeping*].   He had aimed straight at his head
. . . here. . . . Katya fell down fainting, poor darling! . . . And he lay there
terribly frightened, and . . . and asked us to send for a doctor. Soon a
doctor arrived and . . . and saved the poor fellow. . . .

MADAME MERTCHUTKIN.   Your Excellency, couldn't you find another job for my husband?

SHIPUTCHIN.   No, I can't stand it! [*Weeps*] I can't stand it! [*Holds
out both hands to* HIRIN *in despair.*] Turn her out! Turn her out, I implore you!

HIRIN [*going up to* TATYANA ALEXEYEVNA].   Clear out!

SHIPUTCHIN.   Not her, but this . . . this awful woman . . . [*points to*
MADAME MERTCHUTKIN] this one!

HIRIN [*not understanding, to* TATYANA ALEXEYEVNA].   Clear out!
[*Stamps*] Clear out!

TATYANA ALEXEYEVNA.   What? What are you about? Have you gone
off your head?

SHIPUTCHIN.   This is awful! I'm done for! Turn her out! Turn her
out!

HIRIN [*to* TATYANA ALEXEYEVNA].   Get out! I'll smash you! I'll make
mincemeat of you! I'll do something criminal!

TATYANA ALEXEYEVNA [*runs away from him; he runs after her*].   How
dare you! You insolent creature! [*screams*]. Andrey! Save me, Andrey!
[*shrieks*].

SHIPUTCHIN [*runs after them*].   Leave off! I implore you! Hush!
Spare me!

HIRIN [*chasing* MADAME MERTCHUTKIN].   Clear out! Catch her!
Beat her! Cut her throat!

SHIPUTCHIN [*shouts*].   Leave off! I beg you! I implore!

MADAME MERTCHUTKIN.   Holy saints! . . . Holy saints! [*Squeals*]
Holy saints!

TATYANA ALEXEYEVNA [*screams*].   Save me! . . . Ah! Oh! . . . I feel
faint! I feel faint! [*Jumps on to a chair, then falls on the sofa and moans
as though in a swoon.*]

HIRIN [*chasing* MADAME MERTCHUTKIN].   Beat her! Give it her hot!
Kill her!

MADAME MERTCHUTKIN. Oh! Oh! . . . Holy saints! I feel dizzy! Oh!
[*Falls fainting in* SHIPUTCHIN's *arms.*]

[*A knock at the door and a voice behind the scenes:* "The deputation."]

SHIPUTCHIN. Deputation . . . reputation . . . occupation! . . .

HIRIN [*stamps*]. Get out, damn my soul! [*Tucks up his sleeves.*] Let
me get at her! I could do for her!

[*Enter the* Deputation, *consisting of five persons; all are in dress-coats. One holds in his hands the address in a velvet binding, another the silver tankard,* Clerks *look in at the door.* TATYANA
ALEXEYEVNA *on the sofa,* MADAME MERTCHUTKIN *in*
SHIPUTCHIN's *arms, both uttering low moans.*]

ONE OF THE DELEGATES [*reads aloud*]. Dear and highly respected
Andrey Andreyevitch! Casting a retrospective glance over the past of
our financial institution, and taking a mental view of its gradual devel-
opment, we obtain a highly gratifying impression. It is true that in the
early years of its existence the limited amount of our original capital,
the absence of any important transactions, and also the indefiniteness
of our policy, forced into prominence Hamlet's question: To be or not
to be? And at one time voices were even raised in favour of closing the
bank. But then you took the management. Your knowledge, your en-
ergy, and your characteristic tact have been the cause of our extraordi-
nary success and exceptional prosperity. The reputation of the bank
[*coughs*] . . . the reputation of the bank . . .

MADAME MERTCHUTKIN [*moans*]. Oh! Oh!

TATYANA ALEXEYEVNA [*moans*]. Water! Water!

THE DELEGATE [*continues*]. The reputation . . . [*coughs*] the reputation of the bank has been raised by you to such a pinnacle that our
bank may now rival the foremost institutions of the kind in foreign
countries.

SHIPUTCHIN. Deputation . . . reputation . . . occupation! . . . Two
friends one summer evening walked, and sagely of deep matters talked.
. . . Tell me not thy youth is ruined, poisoned by my jealous love. . . .

THE DELEGATE [*continues in confusion*]. Then, turning an objec-
tive eye upon the present we, dear, highly respected Andrey
Andreyevitch . . . [*dropping his voice*] Perhaps later . . . we'd better
come again later . . . [*They walk out in confusion.*]

CURTAIN.

THE PROPOSAL

A JEST IN ONE ACT

Characters in the Play

STEPAN STEPANOVITCH TCHUBUKOV (*a landowner*)
NATALYA STEPANOVNA (*his daughter, age 25*)
IVAN VASSILYEVITCH LOMOV (*a neighbour of* TCHUBUKOV's, *a healthy, well-nourished, but hypochondriacal landowner*)

Drawing-room in TCHUBUKOV's *house.* TCHUBUKOV *and* LOMOV; *the latter enters wearing evening dress and white gloves.*

TCHUBUKOV [*going to meet him*].   My darling, whom do I see? Ivan Vassilyevitch! Delighted! [*shakes hands*]. Well, this is a surprise, dearie. . . . How are you?

LOMOV.   I thank you. And pray, how are you?

TCHUBUKOV.   We are getting on all right, thanks to your prayers, my angel, and all the rest of it. Please sit down. . . . It's too bad, you know, to forget your neighbours, darling. But, my dear, why this ceremoniousness? A swallow-tail, gloves, and all the rest of it! Are you going visiting, my precious?

LOMOV.   No, I have only come to see you, honoured Stepan Stepanovitch.

TCHUBUKOV.   Then why the swallow-tail, my charmer? As though you were paying calls on New Year's Day!

LOMOV.   You see, this is how it is [*takes his arm*]. I have come, honoured Stepan Stepanovitch, to trouble you with a request. I have more than once had the honour of asking for your assistance, and you have always, so to speak—but pardon me, I am agitated. I will have a drink of water, honoured Stepan Stepanovitch [*drinks water*].

TCHUBUKOV [*aside*].   Come to ask for money! I am not going to give it to him. [*To him*] What is it, my beauty?

LOMOV.   You see, Honour Stepanovitch—I beg your pardon, Stepan Honouritch. . . . I am dreadfully agitated, as you see. In short, no one but you can assist me, though, of course, I have done nothing to deserve it, and . . . and . . . have no right to reckon upon your assistance. . . .

TCHUBUKOV.   Oh, don't spin it out, dearie. Come to the point. Well?

LOMOV.   Immediately—in a moment. The fact is that I have come to ask for the hand of your daughter, Natalya Stepanovna.

TCHUBUKOV [*joyfully*].   You precious darling! Ivan Vassilyevitch, say it again! I can't believe my ears.

25

LOMOV. I have the honour to ask . . .

TCHUBUKOV [*interrupting*]. My darling! I am delighted, and all the rest of it. Yes, indeed, and all that sort of thing [*embraces and kisses him*]. I have been hoping for it for ages. It has always been my wish [*sheds a tear*]. And I have always loved you, my angel, as though you were my own son. God give you both love and good counsel, and all the rest of it. I have always wished for it. . . . Why am I standing here like a post? I am stupefied with joy, absolutely stupefied! Oh, from the bottom of my heart. . . . I'll go and call Natasha and that sort of thing.

LOMOV [*touched*]. Honoured Stepan Stepanovitch, what do you think? May I hope that she will accept me?

TCHUBUKOV. A beauty like you, and she not accept you! I'll be bound she is as love-sick as a cat, and all the rest of it. . . . In a minute [*goes out*].

LOMOV. I am cold—I am trembling all over, as though I were in for an examination. The great thing is to make up one's mind. If one thinks about it too long, hesitates, discusses it, waits for one's ideal or for real love, one will never get married. . . . Brr! I am cold. Natalya Stepanovna is an excellent manager, not bad looking, educated— what more do I want? But I am beginning to have noises in my head. I am so upset [*sips water*]. And get married I must. To begin with, I am thirty-five—a critical age, so to speak. And, secondly, I need a regular, well-ordered life. . . . I have valvular disease of the heart, continual palpitations. I am hasty, and am very easily upset. . . . Now, for instance, my lips are quivering and my right eyelid is twitching. . . . But my worst trouble is with sleep. No sooner have I got into bed and just begun to drop asleep, than I have a shooting pain in my left side and a stabbing at my shoulder and my head. . . . I leap up like a madman. I walk about a little and lie down again, but no sooner do I drop off than there's the shooting pain in my side again. And the same thing twenty times over! . . .

[*Enter* NATALYA STEPANOVNA.]

NATALYA. Well, so it's you! Why, and papa said a purchaser had come for the goods! How do you do, Ivan Vassilyevitch?

LOMOV. How do you do, honoured Natalya Stepanovna!

NATALYA. Excuse my apron and *négligé*. We are shelling peas for drying. How is it you have not been to see us for so long? Sit down. [*They sit down.*]. Will you have some lunch?

LOMOV. No, thank you, I have already lunched.

NATALYA. Won't you smoke? Here are the matches. . . . It's a magnificent day, but yesterday it rained so hard that the men did no work at all. How many hay-cocks have you got out? Only fancy, I have been too eager and had the whole meadow mown, and now I am sorry—I am afraid the hay will rot. It would have been better to wait. But what's this? I do believe you have got on your dress-coat! That's something new. Are you going to a ball, or what? And, by the way, you are looking nice. . . . Why are you such a swell, really?

LOMOV [*in agitation*].   You see, honoured Natalya Stepanovna. . . . The fact is that I have made up my mind to ask you to listen to me. . . . Of course, you will be surprised, and even angry, but I . . . It's horribly cold!

NATALYA.   What is it? [*a pause*] Well?

LOMOV.   I will try to be brief. You are aware, honoured Natalya Stepanovna, that from my earliest childhood I had the honour of knowing your family. My late aunt and her husband, from whom, as you know, I inherited the estate, always entertained a profound respect for your papa and your late mamma. The family of the Lomovs and the family of the Tchubukovs have always been on the most friendly and, one may say, intimate terms. Moreover, as you are aware, my land is in close proximity to yours. If you remember, my Volovyi meadows are bounded by your birch copse.

NATALYA.   Excuse my interrupting you. You say "*my* Volovyi meadows." . . . But are they yours?

LOMOV.   Yes, mine.

NATALYA.   Well, what next! The Volovyi meadows are ours, not yours!

LOMOV.   No, they are mine, honoured Natalya Stepanovna.

NATALYA.   That's news to me. How do they come to be yours?

LOMOV.   How do they come to be mine? I am speaking of the Volovyi meadows that run like a wedge between your birch copse and the Charred Swamp.

NATALYA.   Quite so. Those are ours.

LOMOV.   No, you are mistaken, honoured Natalya Stepanovna, they are mine.

NATALYA.   Think what you are saying, Ivan Vassilyevitch! Have they been yours long?

LOMOV.   What do you mean by "long"? As long as I can remember they have always been ours.

NATALYA.   Well, there you must excuse me.

LOMOV.   There is documentary evidence for it, honoured Natalya Stepanovna. The Volovyi meadows were once a matter of dispute, that is true, but now everyone knows that they are mine. And there can be no dispute about it. Kindly consider . . . my aunt's grandmother gave over those meadows to the peasants of your father's grandfather for their use, rent free, for an indefinite period, in return for their firing her bricks. The peasants of your father's grandfather enjoyed the use of the meadows, rent free, for some forty years, and grew used to looking upon them as their own; afterwards, when the settlement came about after the emancipation . . .

NATALYA. It is not at all as you say! Both my grandfather and my great-grandfather considered their land reached to the Charred Swamp—so the Volovyi meadows were ours. I can't understand what there is to argue about. It's really annoying!

LOMOV. I will show you documents, Natalya Stepanovna.

NATALYA. No, you are simply joking, or trying to tease me. . . . A nice sort of surprise! We have owned the land nearly three hundred years, and all of a sudden we are told that the land is not ours! Forgive me, Ivan Vassilyevitch, but I positively cannot believe my ears. . . . I don't care about the meadows. They are not more than fifteen acres, and they are only worth some three hundred roubles, but I am revolted by injustice. You may say what you like, but I cannot endure injustice!

LOMOV. Listen to me, I implore you. The peasants of your father's grandfather, as I had already the honour to inform you, made bricks for my aunt's grandmother. My aunt's grandmother, wishing to do something for them . . .

NATALYA. Grandfather, grandmother, aunt. . . . I don't understand a word of it. The meadows are ours, and that's all about it.

LOMOV. They are mine.

NATALYA. They are ours. If you go on arguing for two days, if you put on fifteen dress-coats, they are still ours, ours, ours! . . . I don't want what's yours, but I don't want to lose what's mine. . . . You can take that as you please!

LOMOV. I do not care about the meadows, Natalya Stepanovna, but it is a matter of principle. If you like, I will make you a present of them.

NATALYA. I might make you a present of them, they are mine. All this is very queer, Ivan Vassilyevitch, to say the least of it. Hitherto we have looked upon you as a good neighbour—a friend. Last year we lent you our threshing-machine, and through that we couldn't finish our threshing till November; and you treat us as if we were gipsies! Make me a present of my own land! Excuse me, but that is not neighbourly. To my thinking it is positively impertinent, if you care to know. . . .

LOMOV. According to you I am a usurper, then? I've never snatched other people's land, madam, and I will allow no one to accuse me of such a thing . . . [*goes rapidly to the decanter and drinks water*]. The Volovyi meadows are mine!

NATALYA. It's not true: they are ours!

LOMOV. They are mine!

NATALYA.   That's not true. I'll prove it. I'll send our mowers to cut the hay there to-day!

LOMOV.   What?

NATALYA.   My labourers will be there to-day.

LOMOV.   I'll kick them out.

NATALYA.   Don't you dare!

LOMOV [*clutches at his heart*].   The Volovyi meadows are mine! Do you understand? Mine!

NATALYA.   Don't shout, please. You can shout and choke with rage when you are at home, if you like; but here I beg you to keep within bounds.

LOMOV.   If it were not for these terrible, agonising palpitations, madam—if it were not for the throbbing in my temples, I should speak to you very differently. [*Shouts*] The Volovyi meadows are mine!

NATALYA.   Ours!

LOMOV.   Mine!

NATALYA.   Ours!

LOMOV.   Mine!

[*Enter* TCHUBUKOV.]

TCHUBUKOV.   What is it? What are you shouting about?

NATALYA.   Papa, explain to this gentleman, please: to whom do the Volovyi meadows belong—to him or to us?

TCHUBUKOV [*to* LOMOV].   My chicken, the meadows are ours.

LOMOV.   But upon my word, Stepan Stepanovitch, how did they come to be yours? Do you, at least, be reasonable. My aunt's grandmother gave over the meadows for temporary gratuitous use to your grandfather's peasants. The peasants made use of the land for forty years and got used to regarding it as their own; but when the Settlement came . . .

TCHUBUKOV.   Allow me, my precious. . . . You forget that the peasants did not pay your grandmother rent and all the rest of it, just because the ownership of the land was in dispute, and so on. . . . And now every dog knows that they are ours. You can't have seen the map.

LOMOV.   I will prove to you that they are mine.

TCHUBUKOV.   You never will, my pet.

LOMOV.   Yes, I will.

TCHUBUKOV.   Why are you shouting, my love? You will prove nothing at all by shouting. I don't desire what is yours, and don't intend to give up what is mine. Why ever should I? If it comes to that, my dear, if you intend to wrangle over the meadows, I would rather give them to the peasants than to you, that I would!

LOMOV.   I don't understand it. What right have you to give away another man's property?

TCHUBUKOV.   Allow me to decide for myself whether I have the right or no. I may say, young man, I am not accustomed to being spoken to in that tone, and all the rest of it. I am twice as old as you are, young man, and I beg you to speak to me without getting excited and all the rest of it.

LOMOV.   Why, you simply take me for a fool and are laughing at me! You call my land yours, and then you expect me to be cool about it and to speak to you properly! That's not the way good neighbours behave, Stepan Stepanovitch. You are not a neighbour, but a usurper!

TCHUBUKOV.   What? What did you say?

NATALYA.   Papa, send the men at once to mow the meadows.

TCHUBUKOV [*to* LOMOV].   What did you say, sir?

NATALYA.   The Volovyi meadows are ours, and I won't give them up. I won't! I won't!

LOMOV.   We will see about that. I'll prove to you in court that they are mine.

TCHUBUKOV.   In court? You can take it into court, sir, and all the rest of it! You can! I know you—you are only waiting for a chance to go to law, and so on. . . . A pettifogging character! All your family were fond of litigation—all of them!

LOMOV.   I beg you not to insult my family. The Lomovs have all been honest men, and not one of them has ever been on his trial for embezzling money like your uncle!

TCHUBUKOV.   Well, you Lomovs have all been mad!

NATALYA.   Everyone of them—everyone of them!

TCHUBUKOV.   Your grandfather was a dipsomaniac, and your youngest aunt, Nastasya Mihailovna, ran away with an architect, and so on.

LOMOV.   And your mother was a hunchback [*clutches at his heart*]. The shooting pain in my side! . . . The blood has rushed to my head. . . . Holy Saints! . . . Water!

TCHUBUKOV.   And your father was a gambler and a glutton!

NATALYA.   And there was no one like your aunt for talking scandal!

LOMOV.   My left leg has all gone numb. . . . And you are an intriguer! . . . Oh, my heart! . . . And it is no secret that before the elections you . . . There are flashes before my eyes! . . . Where is my hat?

NATALYA.   It's mean! It's dishonest! It's disgusting!

TCHUBUKOV.   And you yourself are a viperish, double-faced, mischief-making man. Yes, indeed!

LOMOV.   Here is my hat. . . . My heart! . . . Which way am I to go?

Where's the door? Oh! I believe I am dying! I've lost the use of my leg [*goes towards the door*].

TCHUBUKOV [*calling after him*].   Never set foot within my door again!

NATALYA.   Take it into court! We shall see!

[LOMOV *goes out, staggering.*]

TCHUBUKOV.   Damnation take him! [*walks about in excitement*].

NATALYA.   What a wretch! How is one to believe in good neighbours after that!

TCHUBUKOV.   Blackguard! Scarecrow!

NATALYA.   The object! Collars other people's land—then abuses them!

TCHUBUKOV.   And that noodle—that eyesore—had the face to make a proposal, and all the rest of it. Just fancy, a proposal!

NATALYA.   What proposal?

TCHUBUKOV.   Why, he came here on purpose to propose to you!

NATALYA.   To propose? To me? Why didn't you tell me so before?

TCHUBUKOV.   And he had got himself up in his dress-coat on purpose! The sausage! The shrimp!

NATALYA.   To me? A proposal! Ah! [*She falls into an armchair and moans*] Bring him back! Bring him back! Oh, bring him back!

TCHUBUKOV.   Bring whom back?

NATALYA.   Make haste, make haste! I feel faint! Bring him back! [*Hysterics.*]

TCHUBUKOV.   What is it! What's the matter? [*clutches at his head*] I do have a life of it! I shall shoot myself! I shall hang myself! They'll be the death of me!

NATALYA.   I am dying! Bring him back!

TCHUBUKOV.   T'too! Directly. Don't howl [*runs off*].

NATALYA [*alone, moans*].   What have we done! Bring him back! Bring him back!

TCHUBUKOV [*runs in*].   He is just coming in, and all the rest of it. Damnation take him! Ough! Talk to him yourself, I don't want to. . . .

NATALYA [*moans*].   Bring him back!

TCHUBUKOV [*shouts*].   He is coming, I tell you! What a task it is, O Lord, to be the father of a grown-up daughter! I shall cut my throat! I shall certainly cut my throat! We've abused the man, put him to shame, kicked him out, and it is all your doing—your doing!

NATALYA.   No, it was yours!

TCHUBUKOV.   Oh, it's my fault, so that's it! [LOMOV *appears at the door*]. Well, talk to him yourself [*goes out*].

[*Enter* LOMOV *in a state of collapse.*]

LOMOV.   Fearful palpitations! My leg is numb . . . there's a stitch in my side. . . .

NATALYA.   Forgive us; we were too hasty, Ivan Vassilyevitch. I remember now: the Volovyi meadows really are yours.

LOMOV.   My heart is throbbing frightfully. . . . The meadows are mine. . . . There's a twitching in both my eyelids.

NATALYA.   Yes, they are yours, they are. Sit down. [*They sit down.*] We were wrong.

LOMOV.   I acted from principle. . . . I do not value the land, but I value the principle. . . .

NATALYA.   Just so, the principle. . . . Let us talk of something else.

LOMOV.   Especially as I have proofs. My aunt's grandmother gave the peasants of your father's grandfather . . .

NATALYA.   Enough, enough about that. . . . [*Aside*] I don't know how to begin. [*To him*] Shall you soon be going shooting?

LOMOV.   I expect to go grouse shooting after the harvest, honoured Natalya Stepanovna. Oh! did you hear? Only fancy, I had such a misfortune! My Tracker, whom I think you know, has fallen lame.

NATALYA.   What a pity! How did it happen?

LOMOV.   I don't know. . . . He must have put his paw out of joint, or perhaps some other dog bit it. . . . [*Sighs*] My very best dog, to say nothing of the money I have spent on him! You know I paid Mironov a hundred and twenty-five roubles for him.

NATALYA.   You gave too much, Ivan Vassilyevitch!

LOMOV.   Well, to my mind it was very cheap. He is a delightful dog.

NATALYA.   Father gave eighty-five roubles for his Backer, and Backer is a much better dog than your Tracker.

LOMOV.   Backer a better dog than Tracker? What nonsense! [*laughs*]. Backer a better dog than Tracker!

NATALYA.   Of course he is better. It's true that Backer is young yet— he is hardly a full-grown dog—but for points and cleverness even Voltchanetsky hasn't one to beat him.

LOMOV.   Excuse me, Natalya Stepanovna, but you forget that your Backer has a pug-jaw, and a dog with a pug-jaw is never any good for gripping.

NATALYA.   A pug-jaw! That's the first time I've heard so.

LOMOV.   I assure you the lower jaw is shorter than the upper.

NATALYA.   Why, have you measured?

LOMOV.   Yes. He is all right for coursing, no doubt, but for gripping he'd hardly do.

NATALYA.   In the first place, our Backer is a pedigree dog, son of

Harness and Chisel, but you can't even tell what breed your spotty piebald is. . . . Then he is as old and ugly as a broken-down horse.

LOMOV.   He is old, but I wouldn't exchange him for half a dozen of your Backers. . . . How could I? Tracker is a dog, but Backer—there can be no question about it. Every huntsman has packs and packs of dogs like your Backer. Twenty-five roubles would be a good price for him.

NATALYA.   There is a demon of contradictoriness in you to-day, Ivan Vassilyevitch. First you make out that the meadows are yours, then that your Tracker is a better dog than Backer. I don't like a man to say what he does not think. You know perfectly well that Backer is worth a hundred of your . . . stupid Trackers. Why, then, say the opposite?

LOMOV.   I see, Natalya Stepanovna, that you think I am blind or a fool. Do you understand that your Backer has a pug-jaw?

NATALYA.   It's not true!

LOMOV.   It is!

NATALYA [shouts].   It's not true!

LOMOV.   Why are you shouting, madam?

NATALYA.   Why do you talk nonsense? This is revolting! It's time your Tracker was shot—and you compare him to Backer!

LOMOV.   Excuse me, I cannot continue this argument. I have palpitations.

NATALYA.   I have noticed that men argue most about hunting who know least about it.

LOMOV.   Madam, I beg you to be silent. My heart is bursting. [Shouts] Be silent!

NATALYA.   I will not be silent till you own that Backer is a hundred times better than your Tracker.

LOMOV.   A hundred times worse! Plague take your Backer! My temples . . . my eyes . . . my shoulder. . . .

NATALYA.   There's no need for plague to take your fool of a Tracker—he is as good as dead already.

LOMOV [weeping].   Be silent! My heart is bursting!

NATALYA.   I won't be silent.

[Enter TCHUBUKOV.]

TCHUBUKOV [coming in].   What now?

NATALYA.   Papa, tell me truly, on your conscience, which is the better dog—our Backer or his Tracker?

LOMOV.   Stepan Stepanovitch, I implore you tell me one thing only: has your Backer a pug-jaw or not? Yes or no?

TCHUBUKOV.   And what if he has? It's of no consequence. Anyway, there's no better dog in the whole district, and all the rest of it.

LOMOV.   But my Tracker is better, isn't he? Honestly?

TCHUBUKOV.   Don't excite yourself, my precious. Your Tracker certainly has his good qualities. . . . He is a well-bred dog, has good legs, and is well set-up, and all the rest of it. But the dog, if you care to know, my beauty, has two serious defects: he is old and is snub-nosed.

LOMOV.   Excuse me, I have palpitations. . . . Let us take the facts. . . . If you will kindly remember, at Maruskin's my Tracker kept shoulder to shoulder with the Count's Swinger, while your Backer was a good half-mile behind.

TCHUBUKOV.   Yes, he was, because the Count's huntsman gave him a crack with his whip.

LOMOV.   He deserved it. All the other dogs were after the fox, but Backer got hold of a sheep.

TCHUBUKOV.   That's not true! . . . Darling, I am hot-tempered, and I beg you to drop this conversation. He lashed him because everyone is jealous of another man's dog. . . . Yes, they are all envious! And you are not free from blame on that score either, sir. As soon as you notice, for instance, that someone's dog is better than your Tracker, at once you begin with this and that, and all the rest of it. I remember it all!

LOMOV.   I remember it too!

TCHUBUKOV [*mimics him*].   "I remember it too!" And what do you remember?

LOMOV.   Palpitations! . . . My leg has no feeling in it. I can't . . .

NATALYA [*mimicking him*].   "Palpitations!" . . . A fine sportsman! You ought to be lying on the stove in the kitchen squashing blackbeetles instead of hunting foxes. Palpitations!

TCHUBUKOV.   Yes, you are a fine sportsman, really! With your palpitations you ought to stay at home, instead of jolting in the saddle. It wouldn't matter if you hunted, but you only ride out to wrangle and interfere with other men's dogs and all the rest of it. I am hot-tempered; let us drop this subject. You are not a sportsman at all.

LOMOV.   And you—are you a sportsman? You only go to the hunt to intrigue and make up to the Count. . . . My heart! . . . You are an intriguer!

TCHUBUKOV.   What? Me an intriguer? [*Shouts*] Hold your tongue!

LOMOV.   Intriguer!

TCHUBUKOV.   Milksop! Puppy!

LOMOV.   Old rat! Jesuit!

TCHUBUKOV.   Hold your tongue, or I'll shoot you with a filthy gun like a partridge! Noodle!

LOMOV.   Everyone knows—oh, my heart!—that your wife used to beat you. . . . My leg . . . my forehead . . . my eyes! . . . I shall drop! I shall drop!

TCHUBUKOV.   And you go in terror of your housekeeper!

LOMOV.   Oh, oh, oh! My heart has burst! I can't feel my shoulder—
what has become of my shoulder? I am dying! [*falls into an armchair*].
A doctor! [*swoons*].

TCHUBUKOV.   Puppy! Milksop! Noodle! I feel faint! [*drinks water*].
Faint!

NATALYA.   You are a fine sportsman! You don't know how to sit on
your horse. [*To her father*] Papa, what's the matter with him? Papa!
Look, papa! [*shrieks*]. Ivan Vassilyevitch! He is dead!

TCHUBUKOV.   I feel faint! I can't breathe! Give me air!

NATALYA.   He is dead! [*shakes* LOMOV *by the sleeve*]. Ivan
Vassilyevitch! Ivan Vassilyevitch! What have we done! He is dead! [*falls
into an armchair*]. A doctor! a doctor! [*hysterics*].

TCHUBUKOV.   Och! What is it? What do you want?

NATALYA [*moans*].   He is dead! He is dead!

TCHUBUKOV.   Who is dead? [*looking at* LOMOV] He really is dead!
Holy Saints! Water! A doctor! [*Holds a glass of water to* LOMOV's *lips*]
Drink! . . . No, he won't drink. So he is dead, and all the rest of it. I do
have a life of it! Why don't I put a bullet through my brains? Why is it
I haven't cut my throat? What am I waiting for? Give me a knife! Give
me a pistol! [LOMOV *makes a slight movement*.] I believe he is reviving.
. . . Have a drink of water. That's right.

LOMOV.   Flashes—dizziness—where am I?

TCHUBUKOV.   You'd better make haste and get married—and go to
the devil! She consents [*joins the hands of* LOMOV *and his daughter*].
She accepts you, and all the rest of it. I give you my blessing, and so on.
Only leave me in peace.

LOMOV.   Eh? What? [*getting up*] Who?

TCHUBUKOV.   She accepts you. Well? Kiss each other and . . . be
damned to you!

NATALYA [*moans*].   He is alive! Yes, yes, I accept.

TCHUBUKOV.   Kiss!

LOMOV.   Eh? Whom? [*kisses* NATALYA STEPANOVNA]. Delighted!
Excuse me, what's the point? Oh, yes, I understand! Palpitations . . .
dizziness . . . I am happy, Natalya Stepanovna [*kisses her hand*]. My leg
is numb!

NATALYA.   I . . . I too am happy.

TCHUBUKOV.   It's a load off my heart! Ough!

NATALYA.   But . . . still you must admit now that Tracker is not as
good a dog as Backer.

LOMOV.   He is better!

NATALYA.   He is worse!

TCHUBUKOV.   Well, here's the beginning of family happiness!
Champagne!

LOMOV.   He is better!
NATALYA.   He is not! He is not! He is not!
TCHUBUKOV [*trying to shout them down*].   Champagne! Champagne!

CURTAIN.

THE BEAR

A JEST IN ONE ACT

Characters in the Play

YELENA IVANOVNA POPOV (*a widow with dimples in her cheeks, owner of an estate in the country*)
GRIGORY STEPANITCH SMIRNOV (*a middle-aged landowner*)
LUKA (MADAME POPOV's *old manservant*)

The action takes place in a drawing-room in MADAME POPOV's *house.*

MADAME POPOV (*in deep mourning, keeps her eyes fixed on a photograph*) *and* LUKA.

LUKA.   It's not right, madam. . . . You are simply killing yourself. . . . The cook and the housemaid have gone to the wood to pick strawberries, every breathing thing rejoices, the very cat, even she knows how to enjoy herself and walks about the yard catching birds, while you sit all day indoors as though you were in a nunnery and have no pleasure in anything. Yes, indeed! If you come to think of it, it's nearly a year since you've been out of the house!

MADAME POPOV.   And I shall never go out. . . . Why should I? My life is over. He lies in his grave; I have buried myself within four walls. . . . We are both dead.

LUKA.   Well, there it is! I don't like to hear it. Nikolay Mihailitch is dead, so it had to be, it is God's will. The kingdom of heaven be his! . . . You have grieved, and that's enough; you must know when to stop. You can't weep and wear mourning all your life. I buried my old woman, too, in my time. . . . Well, I was grieved and cried for a month or so, and that was enough for her; but if I had been doleful all my life, it is more than the old woman herself was worth. [*Sighs*] You have forgotten all your neighbours. . . . You don't go out yourself or receive visitors. We live like spiders, if I may say so—we don't see the light of day. The mice have eaten my livery. . . . It's not as though you had no nice people about you: the district is full of gentry. . . . There's a regiment at Ryblovo—the officers are perfect sugar-plums, a sight for sore eyes! And in the camp there is a ball every Friday, and the band plays almost every day. . . . Ah! madam, my dear, you are young and lovely, blooming like a rose—you have only to live and enjoy yourself. . . . Beauty won't last all your life, you know. In another ten years you may want to be as gay as a peacock and dazzle the officers, but then it will be too late. . . .

MADAME POPOV [*resolutely*].   I beg you never to speak like that to me! You know that ever since Nikolay Mihailitch died life has lost all value for me. It appears to you that I am alive, but it is only an appearance! I have taken a vow not to put off this mourning, nor to look upon the world outside as long as I live. . . . Do you hear? May his shade see how I love him! . . . Yes, I know it was no secret to you: he was often unjust to me, cruel and . . . and even unfaithful; but I will be true to the grave, and will show him how I can love. Yonder, on the other side of the grave, he will see me just the same as I was before his death. . . .

LUKA.   Instead of talking like that you had better go for a walk in the garden, or order Toby or Giant to be put into the carriage and go to visit your neighbours. . . .

MADAME POPOV.   Ach! [*weeps*].

LUKA.   Madam! My dear! What is it? Christ be with you!

MADAME POPOV.   He was so fond of Toby! He always used to drive him when he went to the Kortchagins or the Vlassovs. How wonderfully he drove! What grace there was in his figure when he tugged at the reins with all his might! Do you remember? Toby, Toby! Tell them to give him an extra gallon of oats to-day!

LUKA.   Yes, madam.

[*An abrupt ring at the bell.*]

MADAME POPOV [*starts*].   Who is that? Say that I see no one.

LUKA.   Yes, madam [*goes out*].

MADAME POPOV [*looking at the photograph*].   You will see, Nicolas, how I can love and forgive. . . . My love will die only with me when my poor heart leaves off beating [*laughing through her tears*]. And aren't you ashamed? I am a good girl—a true wife. I have locked myself up, and will be true to you to the grave, while you . . . aren't you ashamed, you chubby? You deceived me, you made scenes, left me alone for weeks together. . . .

[LUKA *enters in a fluster.*]

LUKA.   Madam, there is someone asking for you. He wants to see you.

MADAME POPOV.   But didn't you tell him that since my husband's death I see no one?

LUKA.   I did, but he won't listen; he says it is on very urgent business.

MADAME POPOV.   I see no-bo-dy!

LUKA.   I told him so, but . . . he is a regular devil. He swears and just shoves himself into the room . . . he is in the dining-room now.

MADAME POPOV [*irritably*].   Oh, very well! Show him in. How rude!

[LUKA *goes out.*]

MADAME POPOV. How wearisome these people are! What do they want of me? Why should they disturb my peace? [*sighs*]. It seems I shall really have to go into a nunnery . . . [*Ponders*] Yes, a nunnery. . . .

[*Enter* LUKA *with* SMIRNOV.]

SMIRNOV [*as he enters, to* LUKA]. Blockhead, you are too fond of talking! Ass! [*Seeing* MADAME POPOV, *with dignity*] Madam, I have the honour to introduce myself: Grigory Stepanitch Smirnov, landowner and retired lieutenant of artillery. I am compelled to trouble you about a very important matter.

MADAME POPOV [*not offering her hand*]. What can I do for you?

SMIRNOV. Your late husband, whom I had the honour of knowing, owed me twelve hundred roubles on two bills. As I have to-morrow to pay my interest to the land bank, I am obliged to ask you to repay me that sum to-day.

MADAME POPOV. Twelve hundred! . . . And what did my husband owe you that money for?

SMIRNOV. He bought oats from me.

MADAME POPOV [*sighing, to* LUKA]. Don't forget, Luka, to tell them to give Toby an extra gallon of oats [LUKA *goes out. To* SMIRNOV] If Nikolay Mihailitch owed you money, of course I will pay it, but you must please excuse me—I haven't the cash in hand to-day. My steward will be coming back from the town the day after to-morrow, and I will tell him to pay you what is owing; but till then I cannot do what you want. . . . Besides, it is exactly seven months to-day since my husband died, and I am in such a state of mind that I don't feel equal to attending to money matters.

SMIRNOV. And I am in such a state of mind that if I don't pay my interest to-morrow I shall have to put a bullet through my brains. They'll sell up my estate.

MADAME POPOV. The day after to-morrow you shall have the money.

SMIRNOV. I want the money, not the day after to-morrow, but to-day.

MADAME POPOV. Excuse me, I cannot pay you to-day.

SMIRNOV. And I can't wait till the day after to-morrow.

MADAME POPOV. What am I to do if I haven't the money?

SMIRNOV. Then you can't pay it?

MADAME POPOV. I cannot.

SMIRNOV. H'm! Is that your final answer?

MADAME POPOV. Yes.

SMIRNOV. The final? Positively?

MADAME POPOV. Positively.

SMIRNOV.   Very much obliged to you. I'll make a note of it [*shrugs his shoulders*]. And I am expected to keep cool! I met the excise officer on the road just now, and he asked me, "Why are you always so angry, Grigory Stepanitch?" Upon my soul, how can I help being angry? I am in deadly need of money. I set off almost before daylight yesterday morning, I went round to all who owed me money, and not one has paid me! I am as tired as a dog. Goodness knows where I spent the night—in a wretched Jewish pot-house, beside a barrel of vodka. . . . At last I get here, over fifty miles from home, hoping to be paid my money, and all I am offered is a state of mind! How am I to keep my temper?

MADAME POPOV.   I believe I have told you distinctly that when my steward comes back from the town you will be paid.

SMIRNOV.   I have come to see you, and not your steward! What the devil—excuse the expression—do I want with your steward?

MADAME POPOV.   Excuse me, sir, I am not accustomed to such strange expressions and such a tone. I will not listen to you [*goes out quickly*].

SMIRNOV.   Upon my soul! A state of mind! . . . It's seven months since her husband died. . . . But am I to pay the interest, or not? I ask you, am I to pay the interest, or not? To be sure, your husband is dead, and you are in a state of mind, and all sorts of nonsense. Your steward has gone off somewhere—the devil take him!—but what am I to do? Fly away from my creditors on a balloon, or what? Or run and smash my skull against the wall? I went to Gruzdyov—not at home. Yaroshevitch was in hiding. With Kuritsin I had an awful row, and nearly flung him out of a window. Mazutov had a bilious attack, and this one has got a state of mind! Not one of the wretches has paid me! And all because I have been too soft with them—because I am a noodle, a rag, an old woman! I've been too gentle with them. But wait a bit! I'll show you what I can do. I won't let them make a fool of me, damnation take it! I'll stay and stick on here till she does pay. Brr! How cross I feel to-day! I am in such a rage that I'm twitching all over, and I can hardly breathe. . . . Phew! Hang it, I feel positively sick! [*Shouts*] Hi, there!

[*Enter* LUKA.]

LUKA.   What is it?
SMIRNOV.   Give me some kvass or some water.

[LUKA *goes out.*]

SMIRNOV.   Yes, what logic! A man is in deadly need of money—nothing left but to hang himself—and she won't pay because, if you please, she is not equal to attending to money matters! . . . Typical petticoat logic! That is why I never like, and never have liked, talking to women. I'd rather sit on a barrel of gunpowder than talk to a woman! Brr! I am chicken-flesh all over—that feminine creature has put me in such a rage! I have only to see a poetic being like that in the distance for my legs to begin twitching with fury. I feel like shouting "Help!"

[LUKA *enters and gives him water.*]

LUKA.   My lady is unwell and sees no one.
SMIRNOV.   Be off!

[LUKA *goes out.*]

SMIRNOV.   Unwell and sees no one! Very good, you needn't. . . . I'll stay on and sit here till you do pay me. If you are ill a week, I'll stay here for a week. If you are ill for a year, I'll stay for a year. . . . I'll get my own back, my good woman! You won't touch me with your mourning and the dimples in your cheeks. We all know about those dimples! [*Shouts out of window*] Semyon! Take the horses out. We shan't be leaving just directly. I am staying here. Tell them at the stable to give the horses a feed of oats. You've let the left trace horse get its legs into the reins again, you brute! [*Mimicking*] It's a—a—all right. I'll show you if it's all right! [*moves away from the window*]. It's a bad look-out! The heat is insufferable, no one will pay, I had a bad night, and now this mourning female with her state of mind! . . . My head aches. . . . Shall I have some vodka? Perhaps I will. [*Shouts*] Hi, there!

[*Enter* LUKA.]

LUKA.   What is it?
SMIRNOV.   Bring me a glass of vodka. [LUKA *goes out*]. Ough! [*sits down and examines himself*]. I must say, I am a nice sight! Covered with dust, muddy boots, unwashed, uncombed, straws on my waistcoat! The lady thought I was a highwayman, I expect [*yawns*]. . . . It's not quite polite to come into a drawing-room looking like this—but there, it doesn't matter. I am not a visitor—I am a creditor and there is no regulation dress for a creditor.

[*Enter* LUKA.]

LUKA [*giving him vodka*].   You take liberties, sir.
SMIRNOV [*angrily*].   What?
LUKA.   Nothing. I only . . .
SMIRNOV.   To whom are you speaking? Shut up!
LUKA [*aside*].   Well, here's an infliction! It's an ill wind brought him [*goes out*].
SMIRNOV.   Ach, how furious I am! I feel as though I should like to

pound the whole world into powder. . . . I feel positively sick. . . .
[*Shouts*] Hi, there!

[MADAME POPOV *enters, looking down.*]

MADAME POPOV.   Sir, in my solitude I have long been unused to
the human voice, and cannot endure shouting. I beg you most
earnestly not to disturb my peace.

SMIRNOV.   Pay me my money, and I will go.

MADAME POPOV.   I've told you in plain Russian I have no money in
hand at the moment. Wait till the day after to-morrow.

SMIRNOV.   I too had the honour of telling you in plain Russian that
I need the money, not the day after to-morrow, but to-day. If you don't
pay me to-day, I shall have to hang myself to-morrow.

MADAME POPOV.   But what am I to do if I have no money? How
strange it is!

SMIRNOV.   So you won't pay me at once . . . you won't?

MADAME POPOV.   I can't. . . .

SMIRNOV.   In that case I shall stop here, and shall go on staying here
till I get it [*sits down*]. You will pay me the day after to-morrow! Very
good! I shall sit here till the day after to-morrow. I shall sit here like this
. . . [*leaps up*]. I ask you, am I obliged to pay my interest to-morrow, or
not? Or do you think I am joking?

MADAME POPOV.   Sir, I beg you not to shout! This is not a stable.

SMIRNOV.   I am not asking you about a stable. I am asking—have I
got to pay my interest to-morrow, or not?

MADAME POPOV.   You don't know how to behave in the society of
ladies.

SMIRNOV.   Yes, I do know how to behave in the society of ladies.

MADAME POPOV.   No, you don't! You are a coarse, ill-bred man.
Decent people don't speak like that to ladies.

SMIRNOV.   Oh, that's curious! How would you like me to speak to
you? In French, or what? [*Growing angry and speaking with a lisp*]
Madame, je vous prie, how happy I am that you are not paying me my
money. Ach, *pardon* for having troubled you! What a lovely day it is?
And how that mourning suits you! [*bows and scrapes*].

MADAME POPOV.   That's rude and not clever.

SMIRNOV [*mimicking her*].   Rude and not clever! I don't know how
to behave in the society of ladies! Madam, I have seen more women
in my day than you have sparrows. I have fought three duels over
women. I have thrown over twelve women, and nine have thrown me
over. Yes! There was a time when I played the fool—when I was all
sentiment and honey, did the polite, was all bowing and scraping. . . .
I loved and suffered, sighed at the moon, was all thrills and raptures.

. . . I loved passionately, frantically in all sorts of ways, confound me!—chattered like a magpie about the rights of women, spent half my fortune on the tender passion; but now—no, thank you! You won't get round me now. I've had enough. Black eyes, eyes full of passion, crimson lips, dimples, moonlight, whisperings, timid breathing—I would not give a brass farthing for all that, madam! Present company excepted, of course, all women, young and old, are affected, mincing, gossiping, spiteful, liars to the marrow of their bones, trivial, petty, pitiless; their logic is most revolting, and as for this department [*slaps himself on the forehead*]—excuse me for my candour—a sparrow can give points to any philosopher in petticoats! One looks at some poetical creature, all in muslin, an ethereal being, a goddess, a million raptures, but if one peeps into her soul she is the most commonplace crocodile! [*takes hold of the back of a chair; the chair cracks and breaks*]. But what's most revolting is that this crocodile, for some reason, imagines that her *chef-d'œuvre*, her monopoly and privilege, is the tender passion! But, damnation take me, you may hang me on this nail, head downwards, if a woman has ever been capable of loving anyone but a lap-dog! In love all she can do is to whine and whimper. While a man suffers and makes sacrifices, all her love expresses itself in trailing her skirts and trying to keep a tight hold on him. You have the misfortune to be a woman, and so you know a woman's nature from yourself. Tell me honestly, have you ever in your life seen a woman who was sincere, true, and constant? You haven't! None but old women and frights are true and constant. It is easier to find a cat with horns or a white snipe than a constant woman!

MADAME POPOV. Allow me to ask, then, who is true and constant in love according to you? Not man, surely!

SMIRNOV. Yes, man.

MADAME POPOV. Man! [*laughs maliciously*]. Man true and constant in love! That's something new, I must say. [*Hotly*] What right have you to say such a thing? Men true and constant! If it comes to that, I'll tell you that of all the men that I know, or have ever known, the best was my late husband. . . . I loved him passionately, with all my being, as none but a young, spiritual-minded woman can love; I gave him my youth, my life, my happiness, my fortune. He was the breath of my being, the idol I worshipped like a heathen, and—and that best of men deceived me in the most shameless fashion at every step! After his death I found in his table a drawer full of love-letters, and when he was alive—it is dreadful to remember!—he left me alone for weeks at a time. Before my very eyes he made love to other women and deceived me, squandered my money, mocked at my feelings. . . . And in spite of all that I loved him and was faithful to him. . . . What is more, I am still true and faithful to him. I have buried myself within four walls for ever, and I will not cast aside this mourning as long as I live.

SMIRNOV [*laughing contemptuously*]. Mourning! I don't know what you take me for. As though I don't know why you masquerade in black and shut yourself up within four walls! I should think so! It's so mysterious—so romantic! If some young ensign or unfledged poet passes your estate, he will look up at the windows and think, "Here lives the mysterious Tamara who from love for her husband has shut herself within four walls." I know all such tricks.

MADAME POPOV [*flushing crimson*]. What? How dare you say such things to me!

SMIRNOV. You have buried yourself alive, but you have not forgotten to put powder on your face!

MADAME POPOV. How dare you speak to me like that!

SMIRNOV. Don't shout at me, please—I am not your steward! Allow me to call things by their real names. I am not a woman, and am accustomed to say what I think plainly. So don't shout, please.

MADAME POPOV. I am not shouting—it's you who shout. Kindly let me alone!

SMIRNOV. Pay me my money, and I will go away.

MADAME POPOV. I won't give you the money.

SMIRNOV. Yes, you will give it to me!

MADAME POPOV. Just to spite you, I won't give you a farthing! You may as well leave me in peace.

SMIRNOV. I haven't the pleasure of being married or engaged to you, and so please do not make a scene [*sits down*]. I don't like it.

MADAME POPOV [*gasping with indignation*]. You are sitting down?

SMIRNOV. I am.

MADAME POPOV. I beg you to go away.

SMIRNOV. Give me my money! [*Aside*] Oh, how furious I feel!

MADAME POPOV. I don't care to talk to insolent people. Be so good as to take yourself off [*a pause*]. You won't go—you won't?

SMIRNOV. No.

MADAME POPOV. No?

SMIRNOV. No.

MADAME POPOV. Very good, then [*rings the bell*].

[*Enter* LUKA.]

MADAME POPOV. Luka, remove this gentleman.

LUKA [*approaches* SMIRNOV]. Sir, kindly go when you are told. It's no use staying here——

SMIRNOV [*leaping up*]. Hold your tongue! To whom are you speaking? I'll make mincemeat of you!

LUKA [*puts his hands on his heart*].   Holy Saints! [*sinks into an armchair*]. Oh, I feel ill! I feel ill! I can't breathe!

MADAME POPOV.   Where's Dasha? Dasha! [*Shouts*] Dasha! Pelageya! Dasha! [*rings the bell*].

LUKA.   Ach! they've all gone to pick strawberries. There's no one in the house. I feel ill! Water!

MADAME POPOV.   Kindly take yourself off.

SMIRNOV.   Please be more polite.

MADAME POPOV [*clenching her fists and stamping*].   You are a boor! A coarse bear! A bully! A monster!

SMIRNOV.   What? What did you say?

MADAME POPOV.   I said that you were a bear—a monster!

SMIRNOV [*stepping up to her*].   Excuse me, what right have you to insult me?

MADAME POPOV.   Yes, I am insulting you—what of it? Do you suppose I am afraid of you?

SMIRNOV.   And do you think that because you are a poetical creature you have a right to insult people with impunity? Yes? I challenge you!

LUKA.   Saints and holy martyrs! Water!

SMIRNOV.   Pistols!

MADAME POPOV.   If you have got strong fists and can bellow like a bull, do you think I am afraid of you, eh? You bully!

SMIRNOV.   I challenge you! I allow no one to insult me, and it's nothing to me that you are a woman, a weak creature!

MADAME POPOV [*trying to shout him down*].   Bear! bear! bear!

SMIRNOV.   It's time to abandon the prejudice that only men must pay for an insult. If there is to be equality, then let it be equality. Damn it all! I challenge you!

MADAME POPOV.   You want a duel? By all means!

SMIRNOV.   This minute!

MADAME POPOV.   This minute! My husband had pistols. . . . I'll fetch them at once [*goes out and hurriedly returns*]. . . . What pleasure I shall have in putting a bullet through your brazen head! Damnation take you! [*goes out*].

SMIRNOV.   I'll shoot her like a chicken! I am not a boy, I am not a sentimental puppy—feminine frailty means nothing to me.

LUKA.   My good gentleman [*drops on his knees*], for mercy's sake, have pity on an old man! Go away! You've frightened me to death, and now you are going to fight!

SMIRNOV [*not heeding him*].   Fight a duel! That really is equality, emancipation! That does make the sexes equal! I shall shoot her on principle. But what a woman! [*Mimics her*] "Damnation take you! Put a bullet through your brazen head!" . . . What a woman! Her cheeks were flushed, her eyes sparkled. . . . She accepted the challenge! Honour bright, I've never seen anyone like her in my life! . . .

LUKA.   Kind sir, go away! I'll remember you in my prayers!

SMIRNOV.   She is something like a woman! I like that! A real woman! Not a mush of sentiment, but flame, gunpowder, fireworks! I shall be sorry to kill her.

LUKA [*weeps*].   My good sir, go away!

SMIRNOV.   I really like her. I really do! Though she has dimples in her cheeks, I like her! I would forgive her the debt even, and all my anger is gone. . . . A wonderful woman!

[*Enter* MADAME POPOV *with pistols.*]

MADAME POPOV.   Here they are, the pistols. . . . But before we begin the duel, kindly show me how to fire. . . . I've never handled a pistol in my life.

LUKA.   The Lord save us and have mercy upon us! I'll go and look for the gardener and the coachman. What's brought this trouble on us? [*goes out*].

SMIRNOV [*examining the pistols*].   You see, there are several sorts of pistols. . . . There are special duelling pistols, the Mortimer pattern, with capsules. . . . But yours are the Smith-Wesson make, triple action with extractor. . . . They are fine pistols. They are worth at least ninety roubles the brace. . . . You have to hold the revolver like this. [*Aside*] What eyes! what eyes! A ravishing woman!

MADAME POPOV.   Is that right?

SMIRNOV.   Yes, that's it. . . . Then you raise the cock . . . take aim like this. . . . Throw your head a little back! . . . Stretch out your arm full length—that's it. . . . Then with this finger press on that little thing—and that's all. But the chief rule is not to get excited and to take aim slowly. Try not to let your hand shake.

MADAME POPOV.   Very well. It's not convenient to fight indoors; let us go into the garden.

SMIRNOV.   Let us. Only I warn you beforehand I shall fire into the air.

MADAME POPOV.   That's the last straw! Why?

SMIRNOV.   Because . . . because . . . that's my affair.

MADAME POPOV.   You funk it, do you? A-a-ah! No, sir, no wriggling! Kindly follow me. I shall not be satisfied till I have put a bullet through your head—that head that's so hateful to me! Are you funking it?

SMIRNOV.   Yes, I am.

MADAME POPOV.   That's a lie. Why won't you fight?

SMIRNOV.   Because . . . because . . . I like you.

MADAME POPOV [*with a malicious laugh*].   He likes me! He dares to say that he likes me! [*Pointing to the door*] You can go!

SMIRNOV [*in silence puts down the revolver, takes up his cap and is going; near the door he stops. For half a minute they look at each other in silence; then, going irresolutely towards* MADAME POPOV].   I say— are you still angry? I, too, am devilish angry, but you know—how shall I put it? The fact is, you see—it's something like this, to put it plainly. [*Shouts*] Well, it's not my fault that I like you! [*Clutches at the back of the chair; the chair cracks and breaks*] Damnation, what fragile furniture you have! I like you. Do you understand? I—I am almost in love.

MADAME POPOV.   Go away! I hate you!

SMIRNOV.   Good God, what a woman! I have never seen anyone like her. I am lost! I am done for! I am caught like a mouse in a trap!

MADAME POPOV.   Go away, or I'll fire.

SMIRNOV.   Fire away! You can't imagine what joy it would be to die in the sight of those wonderful eyes—to be shot by a revolver held by that little velvety hand! . . . I have gone crazy! Think and decide at once, for if I go away from here, we shall never meet again. Decide! . . . I come of a good family, I am a gentleman, I have ten thousand roubles a year. . . . I can put a bullet through a halfpenny tossed in the air. . . . I've got first-rate horses. . . . Will you be my wife?

MADAME POPOV [*indignant, brandishes the revolver*].   A duel! Let us fight!

SMIRNOV.   I've gone crazy. I can't understand. [*Shouts*] Hi, there! Water!

MADAME POPOV [*shouts*].   I challenge you!

SMIRNOV.   I've gone crazy. I am in love like a boy—like a fool! [*Snatches her hand; she shrieks with pain*] I love you! [*Falls on his knees*] I love you as I have never loved before! I have thrown over twelve women, nine have thrown me over, but I never loved one of them as I love you. . . . I am getting maudlin, I am limp all over, I am a mush! Here I am on my knees like a fool and offering you my hand! . . . It's a shame, a disgrace! I've not been in love for five years. I vowed I wouldn't, and here I am completely bowled over! I offer you my hand. Yes or no? Won't you have it? Very well, you needn't! [*gets up and goes quickly to the door*].

MADAME POPOV.   Stay!

SMIRNOV [*stopping*].   Well?

MADAME POPOV.   Nothing—go! But stay, though—no, go, go! I hate you! Oh, no!—don't go away! Oh, if you knew how angry I am! [*Throws the revolver on the table*] My fingers are numb from the horrid thing. [*Tears her handkerchief in a fury*] Why are you standing there? Go away!

SMIRNOV.   Good-bye!

MADAME POPOV.   Yes, yes, go away! [*Shouts.*] Where are you going? Stay—you can go, though. Oh, how angry I feel! Don't come near me! Don't come near me!

SMIRNOV [*going up to her*].   How angry I am with myself! I am in love like a schoolboy. I've been on my knees—it makes me feel cold all over. . . . [*Rudely*] I love you! As though I wanted to fall in love with you! To-morrow I have to pay my interest, the haymaking has begun, and now you on the top of it all. . . . [*Puts his arm round her waist*] I shall never forgive myself for this!

MADAME POPOV.   Go away! Take your arms away! I—hate you! I chal-challenge you! [A *prolonged kiss.*]

[*Enter* LUKA *with an axe, the gardener with a rake, the coachman with a fork, and labourers with poles.*]

LUKA [*seeing the embracing couple*].   Holy Saints!

[*A pause.*]

MADAME POPOV [*dropping her eyes*].   Luka, tell them in the stable not to give Toby any oats to-day.

CURTAIN.

THE WEDDING

A FARCE IN ONE ACT

Characters in the Play

YEVDOKIM ZAHAROVITCH ZHIGALOV (*retired collegiate registry-clerk*)
NASTASYA TIMOFEYEVNA (*his wife*)
DASHENKA (*their daughter*)
EPAMINOND MAXIMOVITCH APLOMBOV (*her bridegroom*)
FYODOR YAKOVLEVITCH REVUNOV-KARAULOV (*retired naval captain of the second rank*)
ANDREY ANDREYEVITCH NYUNIN (*insurance agent*)
ANNA MARTYNOVNA ZMEYUKIN (*a midwife, about thirty, in a bright magenta dress*)
IVAN MIHAILOVITCH YAT (*a telegraph clerk*)
HARLAMPY SPIRIDONOVITCH DYMBA (*a Greek keeper of a confectioner's shop*)
DMITRY STEPANOVITCH MOZGOVOY (*a sailor in the volunteer fleet*)
BEST MAN, Dancing Gentlemen, Waiters, *etc.*

The action takes place in one of the rooms of a second-class restaurant.

A brilliantly lighted room. A big table laid for supper. Waiters in swallow-tails are busy at the tables. Behind the scenes a band is playing the last figure of the quadrille.

MADAME ZMEYUKIN, YAT, *and the bridegroom's* BEST MAN *walk across the stage.*

MADAME ZMEYUKIN.   No, no, no!

YAT [*following her*].   Have pity on me!

MADAME ZMEYUKIN.   No, no, no!

THE BEST MAN [*hastening after them*].   I say, you can't go on like that! Where are you off to? And the *Grand-rond? Grand-rond*, silvoo-play! [*They go out*].

[*Enter* NASTASYA TIMOFEYEVNA *and* APLOMBOV.]

NASTASYA.   Instead of worrying me, saying all sorts of things, you had much better go and dance.

APLOMBOV.   I am not a Spinoza, to go twirling my legs like a top. I am a practical man and a man of character, and I find no entertainment in idle diversions. But dancing is not what I am talking about. Forgive me, *maman*, but there's a great deal I can't make out in your conduct. For instance, apart from objects of household utility, you promised to give me two lottery tickets with your daughter. Where are they?

NASTASYA.   I've got a shocking headache. . . . It must be the weather. . . . There's going to be a thaw!

APLOMBOV.   Don't try to put me off. I found out to-day that your tickets are pawned. Excuse me, *maman*, no one but an exploiter would do a thing like that. I don't say this from egoisticism—I don't want your lottery tickets—but it's a matter of principle, and I won't allow anyone to do me. I've made your daughter's happiness, and if you don't give me the tickets to-day, I'll make it hot for her! I am a man of honour!

NASTASYA [*looking round the table and counting the places laid*]. One, two, three, four, five . . .

A Waiter. The cook told me to ask you how you will have the ices served: with rum, with Madeira, or with nothing.

Aplombov. With rum. And tell the manager there is not enough wine. Tell him to send some Haut-Sauterne as well. [*To* Nastasya Timofeyevna] You promised, too, and it was an agreed thing, that at supper to-night there should be a general. And where is he, I should like to know?

Nastasya. That's not my fault, my dear.

Aplombov. Who's then?

Nastasya. Andrey Andreyevitch's. He was here yesterday and promised to bring a real general [*sighs*]. I suppose he could not find one anywhere, or he would have brought him. As though we were mean about it! There's nothing we'd grudge for our child's happiness. A general by all means, if you want one. . . .

Aplombov. And another thing. . . . Everybody knows, and so do you, *maman*, that that telegraph clerk Yat was courting Dashenka before I made her an offer. Why have you invited him? Surely you must have known I should dislike it?

Nastasya. Oh, what's your name? Epaminond Maximitch, here you have not been married one day, and already you've worn me out, and Dashenka too, with your talk. And what will it be in a year? You are a trying man, you really are!

Aplombov. You don't like to hear the truth? A-ha! So that's how it is. But you should behave honourably. All I want of you is to be honourable!

[*Couples dancing the* Grand-rond *come in at one door, cross the stage, and go out at another. The first couple are* Dashenka *and the* Best Man, *the last* Yat *and* Madame Zmeyukin. *The last couple drop behind and remain in the room.* Zhigalov *and* Dymba *enter and go up to the table.*]

The Best Man [*shouts*]. Promenade! Messieurs, promenade! [*Behind the scenes*] Promenade!

[*The couples dance out.*]

Yat [*to* Madame Zmeyukin]. Have pity, have pity, enchanting Anna Martynovna!

Madame Zmeyukin. Oh, what a man! . . . I have told you already that I am not in voice to-day.

Yat. I entreat you, do sing! If it's only one note! Have pity! If only one note!

Madame Zmeyukin. You worry me . . . [*sits down and waves her fan*].

YAT. Yes, you really are pitiless! To think of such a cruel creature, if I may use the expression, having such a lovely voice! With such a voice you oughtn't to be a midwife, if you'll allow me to say so, but to sing at public concerts! How divine is your rendering of this phrase, for instance . . . this one . . . [*hums*] . . . "I loved you, love that was in vain" . . . Exquisite!

MADAME ZMEYUKIN [*hums*]. "I loved you, and still it may be love" . . . Is that it?

YAT. Yes, that's it. Exquisite!

MADAME ZMEYUKIN. No, I am not in voice to-day. . . . There, fan me . . . it's hot! [*To* APLOMBOV] Epaminond Maximitch, why are you so melancholy? That's not the thing on your wedding day! You ought to be ashamed, you horrid man! Why, what are you thinking about?

APLOMBOV. Marriage is a serious step. It needs serious consideration from every point of view.

MADAME ZMEYUKIN. What hateful sceptics you all are! I cannot breathe in your society. . . . Give me atmosphere! Do you hear? Give me atmosphere! [*Hums*]

YAT. Exquisite! exquisite!

MADAME ZMEYUKIN. Fan me, fan me! I feel as though my heart were going to burst. . . . Tell me, please, why is it I feel suffocated?

YAT. It's because you are in a sweat. . . .

MADAME ZMEYUKIN. Ough, what vulgarity! Don't dare to use such expressions!

YAT. I beg your pardon! Of course you are used to aristocratic society, if you'll excuse the expression. . . .

MADAME ZMEYUKIN. Oh, let me alone! Give me poetry, raptures! Fan me, fan me! . . .

ZHIGALOV [*to* DYMBA]. Shall we repeat? [*Fills glasses.*] One can drink at any minute. The great thing is not to neglect one's business, Harlampy Spiridonitch. Drink, but keep your wits about you! . . . But as for drinking, why not drink? There's no harm in a drink. . . . To your good health! [*They drink.*] And are there tigers in Greece?

DYMBA. Dere are.

ZHIGALOV. And lions?

DYMBA. Yes, lions too. In Russia dere's noding, but in Greece dere's everyding. Dere I have fader, and uncle, and broders, and here I have noding.

ZHIGALOV. Hm. . . . And are there whales in Greece?

DYMBA. Dere's everyding.

NASTASYA [*to her husband*]. Why are you eating and drinking all anyhow? It's time for everyone to sit down. Don't stick your fork into the tinned lobster. . . . That's for the general. Perhaps he may come yet. . . .

ZHIGALOV.   And are there lobsters in Greece, too?

DYMBA.   Yes . . . dere's everyding dere.

ZHIGALOV.   Hm. . . . And collegiate registry clerks too?

MADAME ZMEYUKIN.   I can imagine what the atmosphere is in Greece!

ZHIGALOV.   And I expect there's a lot of roguery. . . . Greeks are much the same as Armenians or gypsies. They sell you a sponge or a goldfish, and are all agog to fleece you over it. Shall we repeat?

NASTASYA.   What's the good of repeating? It's time we were all sitting down. It's past eleven. . . .

ZHIGALOV.   Well, let us sit down, then. Ladies and gentlemen, pray come to supper! [*Shouts*] Supper! Young people!

NASTASYA.   Dear friends, please come! Sit down!

MADAME ZMEYUKIN [*sitting down at the table*].   Give me poetry! "His restless spirit seeks the storm as though in tempest there were peace!" Give me tempest!

YAT [*aside*].   A remarkable woman! I am in love! head over ears in love!

> [*Enter* DASHENKA, MOZGOVOY, *the* BEST MAN, *gentlemen and ladies. They all sit down noisily; a moment's pause; the band plays a march.*]

MOZGOVOY [*getting up*].   Ladies and gentlemen, I have something to say. . . . We have a great many toasts to drink and speeches to make. Don't let us put them off, but begin at once. Ladies and gentlemen, I propose the toast of the bride and bridegroom!

> [*The band plays a flourish. Shouts of* "Hurrah!" *and clinking of glasses.*]

MOZGOVOY.   It needs sweetening!

ALL.   It needs sweetening!

> [APLOMBOV *and* DASHENKA *kiss.*]

YAT.   Exquisite! exquisite! I must declare, ladies and gentlemen—and it's only paying credit where credit is due—that this room and the establishment generally is magnificent! Superb, enchanting! But, you know, there's one thing wanting to complete it: electric lighting, if you will excuse the expression! In all countries they have electric light now, and only Russia lags behind.

ZHIGALOV [*with an air of profundity*].   Electric light. . . . Hm. . . . But to my mind electric light is nothing but roguery. . . . They stick a bit of coal in, and think they will hoax you with that! No, my good man, if you are going to give us light, don't give us a little bit of coal, but give us something substantial, something solid that you can get hold of! Give us light—you understand—light that's natural and not intellectual!

YAT. If you had seen an electric battery, and what it's made of, you'd think differently.

ZHIGALOV. I don't want to see it. It's roguery. They take simple folks in. . . . Squeeze the last drop out of them. . . . We know all about them. . . . Instead of sticking up for roguery, young man, you had better have a drink and fill other people's glasses. Yes, indeed!

APLOMBOV. I quite agree with you, Pa. What's the use of trotting out these learned subjects? I am quite ready to talk of all sorts of discoveries in the scientific sense, but there's a time for everything! [To DASHENKA] What do you think about it, *ma chère?*

DASHENKA. He wants to show off his learning, and always talks of things no one can understand.

NASTASYA. Thank God, we have lived all our lives without learning, and this is the third daughter we are marrying to a good husband. And if you think we are so uneducated, why do you come to see us? You should go to your learned friends!

YAT. I've always had a respect for your family, Nastasya Timofeyevna, and if I did say a word about electric lighting, it doesn't mean I spoke out of conceit. I am ready enough to have a drink! I have always wished Darya Yevdokimovna a good husband with all the feelings of my heart. It's difficult to find a good husband nowadays, Nastasya Timofeyevna. Nowadays everybody is keen on marrying for money. . . .

APLOMBOV. That's a hint at me!

YAT [scared]. Not the slightest hint intended. . . . I was not speaking of present company. . . . I meant it as a general remark. . . . Upon my word! Everyone knows you are marrying for love. . . . The dowry is not worth talking about!

NASTASYA. Not worth talking about, isn't it? You mind what you are saying, sir. Besides a thousand roubles in cash, we are giving three pelisses, the bedding and all the furniture. You try and find a dowry to match that!

YAT. I didn't mean anything. . . . The furniture is certainly nice . . . and . . . and the pelisses, of course; I only spoke in the sense that they're offended as though I'd dropped a hint.

NASTASYA. Well, you shouldn't drop hints. It's out of regard for your parents we asked you to the wedding, and you keep saying all sorts of things. And if you knew that Epaminond Maximovitch was after her money, why didn't you speak before? [*Tearfully*] I have reared and nurtured her. . . . I've watched over her like a diamond or an emerald, my sweet child. . . .

APLOMBOV. And you believe him? Much obliged, I am sure! Very much obliged. [*To* YAT] And as for you, Mr. Yat, though you are a friend, I won't allow you to behave so disgracefully in other people's houses! Kindly take yourself off!

YAT. What do you mean?

APLOMBOV. I could wish you were as much of a gentleman as I am! In fact, kindly take yourself off.

[*The band plays a flourish.*]

GENTLEMEN [*to* APLOMBOV]. Oh, stop it! Leave off! It doesn't matter! Sit down! Let him alone!

YAT. I wasn't saying anything . . . why, I . . . In fact, I don't understand it. . . . Certainly, I'll go. . . . But first pay me the five roubles you borrowed from me a year ago to buy yourself a piqué waistcoat; excuse the expression. I'll have another drink and I'll . . . I'll go, only first pay me what you owe me.

GENTLEMEN. Come, stop it, stop it! That's enough! Making such a fuss about nothing!

THE BEST MAN [*shouts*]. To the health of the bride's parents, Yevdokim Zaharitch and Nastasya Timofeyevna!

[*The band plays a flourish. Shouts of* "Hurrah!"]

ZHIGALOV [*touched, bows in all directions*]. Thank you, good friends! I am very grateful to you for not forgetting us and not being too proud to come! . . . Don't think that I am a knave or that it's roguery. I speak merely as I feel! In the simplicity of my heart! For my friends I grudge nothing! I thank you sincerely! [*Kisses those near him.*]

DASHENKA [*to her mother*]. Ma, why are you crying? I am so happy.

APLOMBOV. Maman is upset at the approaching separation. But I would advise her to think over our conversation.

YAT. Don't cry, Nastasya Timofeyevna! Think what human tears are! Neurotic weakness, that's all!

ZHIGALOV. And are there mushrooms in Greece?

DYMBA. Yes, dere is everyding dere.

ZHIGALOV. But, I bet, there are no brown ones, like ours.

DYMBA. Yes, dere are.

MOZGOVOY. Harlampy Spiridonitch, it's your turn to make a speech! Ladies and gentlemen, let him make a speech!

ALL. A speech! a speech! It's your turn.

DYMBA. Why? What for? I not understand what it is. . . .

MADAME ZMEYUKIN.   No, no! Don't dare to refuse! It's your turn! Get up!

DYMBA [*stands up, in confusion*].   I can say dis. . . . Dere's Russia and dere's Greece. Dere's people in Russia and dere's people in Greece. . . . And *caravies* floating on de sea, dat is in Russia, ships, and on de earth de different railways. I know very well. . . . We Greeks, you Russians, and not want noding. I can tell you . . . dere's Russia and dere's Greece.

[*Enter* NYUNIN.]

NYUNIN.   Stay, ladies and gentlemen, don't eat yet! Wait a bit! Nastasya Timofeyevna, one minute; Come this way! [*Draws* NASTASYA TIMOFEYEVNA *aside, breathlessly.*] I say, the general is just coming. . . . At last I've got hold of him. . . . I am simply worn out. . . . A real general, so dignified, elderly, eighty I should think, or perhaps ninety. . . .

NASTASYA.   When is he coming?

NYUNIN.   This minute! You will be grateful to me to the end of your days. Not a general but a peach, a Boulanger! Not a common general, not an infantry man, but a naval one! In grade he is a captain of the second rank, but in their reckoning, in the fleet, it's equal to a major-general, or, in the civil service, to an actual civil councillor. It's exactly the same; higher, in fact.

NASTASYA.   You are not deceiving me, Andryushenka?

NYUNIN.   What next! Am I a swindler? Set your mind at rest.

NASTASYA [*with a sigh*].   I don't want to spend my money for nothing, Andryushenka. . . .

NYUNIN.   Set your mind at rest! He is a perfect picture of a general! [*Raising his voice*] I said to him: "You have quite forgotten us, your Excellency! It's too bad, your Excellency, to forget your old friends! Nastasya Timofeyevna," I said, "is quite huffy!" [*Goes to the table and sits down.*] And he said to me: "Upon my soul, my boy, how can I go when I don't know the bridegroom?" "What next, your Excellency! why stand on ceremony? The bridegroom is a splendid fellow, an open-hearted chap. He is a valuer in a pawnbroker's shop," I told him, "but don't imagine, your Excellency, that he is a paltry beggar or a cad. Even well-born ladies serve in pawnshops nowadays." He slapped me on the shoulder, we each had a Havana cigar, and here he is coming now. . . . Wait a minute, ladies and gentlemen, don't eat. . . .

APLOMBOV.   And when will he be here?

NYUNIN.   This minute. He was putting on his goloshes when I came away.

APLOMBOV.   Then we must tell them to play a march.

NYUNIN [*shouts*]. Hey, bandmaster! A march! [*The band plays a march for a minute.*]

A WAITER [*announces*]. Mr. Revunov-Karaulov!

> [ZHIGALOV, NASTASYA TIMOFEYEVNA, *and* NYUNIN *hasten to meet him. Enter* REVUNOV-KARAULOV.]

NASTASYA [*bowing*]. You are very welcome, your Excellency! Delighted to see you!

REVUNOV. Delighted!

ZHIGALOV. We are not distinguished or wealthy people, your Excellency, we are plain folks; but don't think there's any roguery on our part. We grudge nothing for nice people, nothing is too good for them. You are very welcome!

REVUNOV. Delighted!

NYUNIN. Allow me to introduce, your Excellency! The bridegroom Epaminond Maximitch Aplombov, with his newborn. . . . I mean newly married bride! Ivan Mihailitch Yat, of the telegraph department. Harlampy Spiridonitch Dymba, a foreigner of Greek extraction, in the confectionery line! Osip Lukitch Babelmandebsky! and so on . . . and so on. . . . The rest are not much account. Sit down, your Excellency.

REVUNOV. Delighted! Excuse me, ladies and gentlemen, I want to say a couple of words to Andryusha [*leads* NYUNIN *aside*]. I feel rather awkward, my boy. . . . Why do you call me "your Excellency"? Why, I am not a general! A captain of the second rank; it isn't even as good as a colonel.

NYUNIN [*speaks into his ear as to a deaf man*]. I know, but, Fyodor Yakovlevitch, be so good as to let us say "your Excellency"! They are a patriarchal family here, you know; they honour their betters, and like to show respect where respect is due. . . .

REVUNOV. Well, if that's how it is, of course . . . [*going to the table*]. Delighted!

NASTASYA. Sit down, your Excellency! Do us the honour! What will you take, your Excellency? Only you must excuse us, you are accustomed to dainty fare at home, while we are plain people!

REVUNOV [*not hearing*]. What? Hm. . . . Yes. . . . [*a pause*]. Yes. . . . In old days people all lived plainly and were satisfied. I am a man of rank in the service, but I live plainly. . . . Andryusha came to me to-day and invited me here to the wedding. "How can I go," said I, "when I don't know them? That would be awkward!" But, he said, "They are plain people, a patriarchal family, always glad to see a visitor." "Oh well, of course if that is how it is . . . Why not? I am delighted. It's dull for me at home all alone, and if my being at the wedding can give pleasure to anyone, well, by all means," I said.

ZHIGALOV.   So it was in the kindness of your heart, your Excellency? I honour you! I am a plain man, with no sort of roguery about me, and I respect those that are the same. Pray take something, your Excellency.

APLOMBOV.   Have you long left the service, your Excellency?

REVUNOV.   Eh? Yes, yes . . . to be sure. That's true. Yes. . . . But how is this? The herring is bitter and the bread is bitter, I can't eat it.

ALL.   It needs sweetening!

[APLOMBOV *and* DASHENKA *kiss.*]

REVUNOV.   He-he-he! . . . Your health! [*a pause*] Yes. . . . In old days everything was plain, and everyone was satisfied. . . . I like plain ways. . . . I am an old man. Of course, I retired from the service in 1865. I am seventy-two. . . . Yes. In old days to be sure, they liked, too, on occasion to make a show, but . . . [*seeing* MOZGOVOY]. You . . . er . . . are a sailor, aren't you?

MOZGOVOY.   Yes, sir.

REVUNOV.   Aha! . . . To be sure. . . . Yes. . . . The naval service was always a hard one. You've something to think about and rack your brains over. Every trivial word has, so to say, a special meaning. For instance: Mast-hands, to the top-sail lifts and the mainsail braces! What does that mean? A sailor understands, no fear about that! Ha-ha! It's as hard as any mathematics.

NYUNIN.   To the health of his Excellency, Fyodor Yakovlevitch Revunov-Karaulov!

[*Band plays a flourish.*]

ALL.   Hurrah!

YAT.   Well, your Excellency, you've just been pleased to tell us something about the difficulties of the naval service. But is the telegraph service any easier? Nowadays, your Excellency, no one can go in for the telegraph service unless he can read and write French and German. But the hardest job for us is transmitting the telegrams! It's awfully difficult! Just listen [*taps with his fork on the table, imitating the telegraph code*].

REVUNOV.   And what does that mean?

YAT.   That means: I respect you, your Excellency, for your noble qualities. Do you suppose that's easy? And now listen [*taps*].

REVUNOV.   A little louder. . . . I don't hear.

YAT.   That means: Madam, how happy I am to hold you in my arms.

REVUNOV.   What madam are you talking about? Yes . . . [*to* MOZGOVOY]. And now if you are sailing with a strong wind and want to hoist the top-gallant sail and the royal, then you must shout: Sail hands, on the cross-trees to the top-gallant sail and the royal sail! . . . and while they pay out the sails on the yards below, they are at the top-gallant and royal halyards, stays and braces. . . .

THE BEST MAN [*getting up*]. Ladies and gentle . . .

REVUNOV [*interrupting*]. Yes . . . there are all sorts of orders to be given. . . . Yes. . . . Top-gallant sheets and royal sheets taut, let go the lifts! Sounds fine, doesn't it? But what does it mean? Oh, it's very simple. They pull the top-gallant and royal sheets and raise the lifts. . . . All at once! And at the same time as they raise them, level the royal sheets and the royal lifts, and, where necessary, slacken the braces of those sails, and when the sheets are taut and all the lifts have been raised to their places, the top-gallant braces and the royal braces are taut and the yards are turned the way of the wind. . . .

NYUNIN [*to* REVUNOV]. Fyodor Yakovlevitch! our hostess begs you to talk of something else. Our guests can't understand this, they are bored. . . .

REVUNOV. What? Who is bored? [*To* MOZGOVOY] Young man! Now, if the ship is lying with the wind on the starboard tack, under full sail, and you want to bring her round before the wind, what order must you give? Why, pipe all hands on deck, bring her round before the wind.

NYUNIN. Fyodor Yakovlevitch, that's enough, eat your supper!

REVUNOV. As soon as they have all run up, you give the command at once: Stand to your places, bring her round before the wind! Ah, what a life! You give the command and see the sailors run like lightning to their places and pull the stays and the braces, then you can't help shouting, Bravo, lads! [*Chokes and coughs.*]

THE BEST MAN [*hastening to take advantage of the ensuing pause*]. On this, so to speak, festive occasion, on which we, all gathered together here, to do honour to our beloved . . .

REVUNOV [*interrupting*]. Yes! And you have to remember all that! For instance: let out the fore-top-sail-sheet, top-gallant-sail sheet! . . .

THE BEST MAN [*offended*]. Why does he interrupt? At this rate we shan't get through a single speech!

NASTASYA. We are ignorant people, your Excellency, we don't understand a word of all this. If you would tell us something that would amuse . . .

REVUNOV [*not hearing*]. Thank you, I have had some. Did you say goose? Thank you. . . . Yes. I was recalling old days. It's a jolly life, young man! You float over the sea without a care in your heart and . . . [*In a shaking voice*] Do you remember the excitement of tacking? What sailor isn't fired by the thought of that manœuvre! Why, as soon

as the command is given: Pipe all hands on deck, it's like an electric
shock running through them all. From the commanding officer to the
lowest sailor they are all in a flutter. . . .

MADAME ZMEYUKIN.   I am bored, I am bored! [A general murmur].

REVUNOV [not hearing].   Thank you, I have had some. [With en-
thusiasm] Everyone is ready and all eyes are fixed on the senior officer.
. . . "Fore-topsail and mainsail braces to starboard, mizzen-braces to lar-
board, counter-braces to port," shouts the senior officer..Every order is
carried out instantly. "Slacken fore-sheet and jib-stay . . . right to starboard!" [Gets up.] Then the ship rolls to the wind and the sails begin
to flap. The senior officer shouts "To the braces! to the braces! look
alive!" While he fixes his eyes on the topsail and when at last it begins
to flap, that is, when the ship begins to turn, a terrific yell is heard:
"Loose the mainsail-stays, let go the braces!" Then everything is flying
and creaking—a regular tower of Babel! it's all done without a break.
The ship is turned!

NASTASYA [flaring up].   For all you are a general, you've no manners! You should be ashamed at your age!

REVUNOV.   Greengage? No, I have not had any. . . . Thank you.

NASTASYA [aloud].   I say, you ought to be ashamed at your age! You
are a general, but you have no manners!

NYUNIN [in confusion].   Come, friends! . . . why make a fuss? . . .
really.

REVUNOV.   To begin with, I am not a general, but a captain of the
second rank, which corresponds to a lieutenant-colonel of military
rank.

NASTASYA.   If you are not a general, what did you take the money
for? We did not pay you money to be rude to us!

REVUNOV [in perplexity].   What money?

NASTASYA.   You know very well what money. You got the twenty-five
roubles from Andrey Andreyevitch right enough . . . [to NYUNIN]. It's
too bad of you, Andryusha! I didn't ask you to engage a fellow like this.

NYUNIN.   Oh, come. . . . Drop it! Why make a fuss?

REVUNOV.   Engaged . . . Paid . . . What does it mean?

APLOMBOV.   Allow me. . . . You've received twenty-five roubles from
Andrey Andreyevitch, haven't you?

REVUNOV.   Twenty-five roubles? [Grasping the situation] So that's
how it is! Now I understand it! What a dirty trick! What a dirty trick!

APLOMBOV.   Well, you had the money, hadn't you?

REVUNOV.   I've had no money! Get away with you! [Gets up from
the table.] What a dirty trick! What a mean trick! To insult an old man
like this—a sailor—an officer who has seen honourable service! . . . If
these were decent people I might challenge someone to a duel, but as

it is, what can I do? [*Distractedly*] Where is the door? Which way do I go? Waiter! show me out! Waiter! [*Going*] What a mean trick! What a dirty trick! [*Goes out.*]

NASTASYA.   Andryusha, where is that twenty-five roubles, then?

NYUNIN.   Oh, don't make a fuss about such a trifle! As though it matters! Here everyone is rejoicing, while you keep on about this silly business. [*Shouts*] To the health of the happy pair! Band, a march! [*The band plays a march.*] To the health of the happy pair!

MADAME ZMEYUKIN.   I am stifling! Give me atmosphere! At your side I am suffocated!

YAT [*delighted*].   Exquisite creature!

[*Hubbub.*]

THE BEST MAN [*trying to shout above the rest*].   Ladies and gentlemen! On this, so to say, festive occasion . . .

CURTAIN.

DOVER·THRIFT·EDITIONS

FICTION

MADAME BOVARY, Gustave Flaubert. 256pp. 29257-6 $2.00

WHERE ANGELS FEAR TO TREAD, E. M. Forster. 128pp. (Available in U.S. only) 27791-7 $1.50

A ROOM WITH A VIEW, E. M. Forster. 176pp. (Available in U.S. only) 28467-0 $2.00

THE OVERCOAT AND OTHER STORIES, Nikolai Gogol. 112pp. 27057-2 $1.50

GREAT GHOST STORIES, John Grafton (ed.). 112pp. 27270-2 $1.00

"THE MOONLIT ROAD" AND OTHER GHOST AND HORROR STORIES, Ambrose Bierce (John Grafton, ed.) 96pp. 40056-5 $1.00

THE MABINOGION, Lady Charlotte E. Guest. 192pp. 29541-9 $2.00

WINESBURG, OHIO, Sherwood Anderson. 160pp. 28269-4 $2.00

THE LUCK OF ROARING CAMP AND OTHER STORIES, Bret Harte. 96pp. 27271-0 $1.00

THIS SIDE OF PARADISE, F. Scott Fitzgerald. 208pp. 28999-0 $2.00

"THE DIAMOND AS BIG AS THE RITZ" AND OTHER STORIES, F. Scott Fitzgerald. 29991-0 $2.00

THE SCARLET LETTER, Nathaniel Hawthorne. 192pp. 28048-9 $2.00

YOUNG GOODMAN BROWN AND OTHER STORIES, Nathaniel Hawthorne. 128pp. 27060-2 $1.00

THE GIFT OF THE MAGI AND OTHER SHORT STORIES, O. Henry. 96pp. 27061-0 $1.00

THE NUTCRACKER AND THE GOLDEN POT, E. T. A. Hoffmann. 128pp. 27806-9 $1.00

THE BEAST IN THE JUNGLE AND OTHER STORIES, Henry James. 128pp. 27552-3 $1.00

DAISY MILLER, Henry James. 64pp. 28773-4 $1.00

WASHINGTON SQUARE, Henry James. 176pp. 40431-5 $2.00

THE TURN OF THE SCREW, Henry James. 96pp. 26684-2 $1.00

DUBLINERS, James Joyce. 160pp. 26870-5 $1.00

A PORTRAIT OF THE ARTIST AS A YOUNG MAN, James Joyce. 192pp. 28050-0 $2.00

DEATH IN VENICE, Thomas Mann. 96pp. (Available in U.S. only) 28714-9 $1.00

THE METAMORPHOSIS AND OTHER STORIES, Franz Kafka. 96pp. 29030-1 $1.50

THE MAN WHO WOULD BE KING AND OTHER STORIES, Rudyard Kipling. 128pp. 28051-9 $1.50

SREDNI VASHTAR AND OTHER STORIES, Saki (H. H. Munro). 96pp. 28521-9 $1.00

THE OIL JAR AND OTHER STORIES, Luigi Pirandello. 96pp. 28459-X $1.00

SELECTED SHORT STORIES, D. H. Lawrence. 128pp. 27794-1 $1.00

GREEN TEA AND OTHER GHOST STORIES, J. Sheridan LeFanu. 96pp. 27795-X $1.00

SHORT STORIES, Theodore Dreiser. 112pp. 28215-5 $1.50

THE CALL OF THE WILD, Jack London. 64pp. 26472-6 $1.00

FIVE GREAT SHORT STORIES, Jack London. 96pp. 27063-7 $1.00

WHITE FANG, Jack London. 160pp. 26968-X $1.00

THE NECKLACE AND OTHER SHORT STORIES, Guy de Maupassant. 128pp. 27064-5 $1.00

BARTLEBY AND BENITO CERENO, Herman Melville. 112pp. 26473-4 $1.00

THE GOLD-BUG AND OTHER TALES, Edgar Allan Poe. 128pp. 26875-6 $1.00

TALES OF TERROR AND DETECTION, Edgar Allan Poe. 96pp. 28744-0 $1.00

DETECTION BY GASLIGHT, Douglas G. Greene (ed.). 272pp. 29928-7 $2.00

THE THIRTY-NINE STEPS, John Buchan. 96pp. 28201-5 $1.50

THE QUEEN OF SPADES AND OTHER STORIES, Alexander Pushkin. 128pp. 28054-3 $1.50

FIRST LOVE AND DIARY OF A SUPERFLUOUS MAN, Ivan Turgenev. 96pp. 28775-0 $1.50

FATHERS AND SONS, Ivan Turgenev. 176pp. 40073-5 $2.00

FRANKENSTEIN, Mary Shelley. 176pp. 28211-2 $1.00

THREE LIVES, Gertrude Stein. 176pp. (Available in U.S. only) 28059-4 $2.00

DOVER·THRIFT·EDITIONS

FICTION

THE STRANGE CASE OF DR. JEKYLL AND MR. HYDE, Robert Louis Stevenson. 64pp. 26688-5 $1.00

TREASURE ISLAND, Robert Louis Stevenson. 160pp. 27559-0 $1.50

THE LOST WORLD, Arthur Conan Doyle. 176pp. 40060-3 $1.50

GULLIVER'S TRAVELS, Jonathan Swift. 240pp. 29273-8 $2.00

ROBINSON CRUSOE, Daniel Defoe. 288pp. 40427-7 $2.00

THE KREUTZER SONATA AND OTHER SHORT STORIES, Leo Tolstoy. 144pp. 27805-0 $1.50

THE IMMORALIST, André Gide. 112pp. (Available in U.S. only) 29237-1 $1.50

ADVENTURES OF HUCKLEBERRY FINN, Mark Twain. 224pp. 28061-6 $2.00

THE ADVENTURES OF TOM SAWYER, Mark Twain. 192pp. 40077-8 $2.00

THE MYSTERIOUS STRANGER AND OTHER STORIES, Mark Twain. 128pp. 27069-6 $1.00

HUMOROUS STORIES AND SKETCHES, Mark Twain. 80pp. 29279-7 $1.00

YOU KNOW ME AL, Ring Lardner. 128pp. 28513-8 $1.00

MOLL FLANDERS, Daniel Defoe. 256pp. 29093-X $2.00

CANDIDE, Voltaire (François-Marie Arouet). 112pp. 26689-3 $1.00

"THE COUNTRY OF THE BLIND" AND OTHER SCIENCE-FICTION STORIES, H. G. Wells. 160pp. (Available in U.S. only) 29569-9 $1.00

THE ISLAND OF DR. MOREAU, H. G. Wells. (Available in U.S. only) 29027-1 $1.00

THE INVISIBLE MAN, H. G. Wells. 112pp. (Available in U.S. only) 27071-8 $1.00

THE TIME MACHINE, H. G. Wells. 80pp. (Available in U.S. only) 28472-7 $1.00

LOOKING BACKWARD, Edward Bellamy. 160pp. 29038-7 $2.00

THE WAR OF THE WORLDS, H. G. Wells. 160pp. (Available in U.S. only) 29506-0 $1.00

ETHAN FROME, Edith Wharton. 96pp. 26690-7 $1.00

SHORT STORIES, Edith Wharton. 128pp. 28235-X $1.00

THE AGE OF INNOCENCE, Edith Wharton. 288pp. 29803-5 $2.00

THE MOON AND SIXPENCE, W. Somerset Maugham. 176pp. (Available in U.S. only) 28731-9 $2.00

THE PICTURE OF DORIAN GRAY, Oscar Wilde. 192pp. 27807-7 $1.50

MONDAY OR TUESDAY: Eight Stories, Virginia Woolf. 64pp. (Available in U.S. only) 29453-6 $1.00

JACOB'S ROOM, Virginia Woolf. 144pp. (Available in U.S. only) 40109-X $1.50

NONFICTION

THE DEVIL'S DICTIONARY, Ambrose Bierce. 144pp. 27542-6 $1.00

DE PROFUNDIS, Oscar Wilde. 64pp. 29308-4 $1.00

OSCAR WILDE'S WIT AND WISDOM: A Book of Quotations, Oscar Wilde. 64pp. 40146-4 $1.00

THE SOULS OF BLACK FOLK, W. E. B. Du Bois. 176pp. 28041-1 $2.00

NARRATIVE OF THE LIFE OF FREDERICK DOUGLASS, Frederick Douglass. 96pp. 28499-9 $1.00

NARRATIVE OF SOJOURNER TRUTH, Sojourner Truth. 80pp. 29899-X $1.00

UP FROM SLAVERY, Booker T. Washington. 160pp. 28738-6 $2.00

A VINDICATION OF THE RIGHTS OF WOMAN, Mary Wollstonecraft. 224pp. 29036-0 $2.00

THE SUBJECTION OF WOMEN, John Stuart Mill. 112pp. 29601-6 $1.50

TAO TE CHING, Lao Tze. 112pp. 29792-6 $1.00

THE ANALECTS, Confucius. 128pp. 28484-0 $2.00

SELF-RELIANCE AND OTHER ESSAYS, Ralph Waldo Emerson. 128pp. 27790-9 $1.00

SELECTED ESSAYS, Michel de Montaigne. 96pp. 29109-X $1.50

DOVER·THRIFT·EDITIONS

NONFICTION

A MODEST PROPOSAL AND OTHER SATIRICAL WORKS, Jonathan Swift. 64pp. 28759-9 $1.00
UTOPIA, Sir Thomas More. 96pp. 29583-4 $1.50
THE AUTOBIOGRAPHY OF BENJAMIN FRANKLIN, Benjamin Franklin. 144pp. 29073-5 $1.50
COMMON SENSE, Thomas Paine. 64pp. 29602-4 $1.00
THE STORY OF MY LIFE, Helen Keller. 80pp. 29249-5 $1.00
GREAT SPEECHES, Abraham Lincoln. 112pp. 26872-1 $1.00
THE PRINCE, Niccolò Machiavelli. 80pp. 27274-5 $1.00
PRAGMATISM, William James. 128pp. 28270-8 $1.50
TOTEM AND TABOO, Sigmund Freud. 176pp. (Available in U.S. only) 40434-X $2.00
POETICS, Aristotle. 64pp. 29577-X $1.00
NICOMACHEAN ETHICS, Aristotle. 256pp. 40096-4 $2.00
MEDITATIONS, Marcus Aurelius. 128pp. 29823-X $1.50
SYMPOSIUM AND PHAEDRUS, Plato. 96pp. 27798-4 $1.50
THE TRIAL AND DEATH OF SOCRATES: Four Dialogues, Plato. 128pp. 27066-1 $1.00
THE BIRTH OF TRAGEDY, Friedrich Nietzsche. 96pp. 28515-4 $1.50
BEYOND GOOD AND EVIL: Prelude to a Philosophy of the Future, Friedrich Nietzsche. 176pp. 29868-X $1.50
CONFESSIONS OF AN ENGLISH OPIUM EATER, Thomas De Quincey. 80pp. 28742-4 $1.00
CIVIL DISOBEDIENCE AND OTHER ESSAYS, Henry David Thoreau. 96pp. 27563-9 $1.00
SELECTIONS FROM THE JOURNALS (Edited by Walter Harding), Herny David Thoreau. 96pp. 28760-2 $1.00
WALDEN; OR, LIFE IN THE WOODS, Henry David Thoreau. 224pp. 28495-6 $2.00
THE LAND OF LITTLE RAIN, Mary Austin. 96pp. 29037-9 $1.50
THE THEORY OF THE LEISURE CLASS, Thorstein Veblen. 256pp. 28062-4 $2.00

PLAYS

PROMETHEUS BOUND, Aeschylus. 64pp. 28762-9 $1.00
THE ORESTEIA TRILOGY: Agamemnon, The Libation-Bearers and The Furies, Aeschylus. 160pp. 29242-8 $1.50
LYSISTRATA, Aristophanes. 64pp. 28225-2 $1.00
WHAT EVERY WOMAN KNOWS, James Barrie. 80pp. (Available in U.S. only) 29578-8 $1.50
THE CHERRY ORCHARD, Anton Chekhov. 64pp. 26682-6 $1.00
THE THREE SISTERS, Anton Chekhov. 64pp. 27544-2 $1.00
UNCLE VANYA, Anton Chekhov. 64pp. 40159-6 $1.50
THE INSPECTOR GENERAL, Nikolai Gogol. 80pp. 28500-6 $1.50
THE WAY OF THE WORLD, William Congreve. 80pp. 27787-9 $1.50
BACCHAE, Euripides. 64pp. 29580-X $1.00
MEDEA, Euripides. 64pp. 27548-5 $1.00
THE MIKADO, William Schwenck Gilbert. 64pp. 27268-0 $1.50
FAUST, PART ONE, Johann Wolfgang von Goethe. 192pp. 28046-2 $2.00
SHE STOOPS TO CONQUER, Oliver Goldsmith. 80pp. 26867-5 $1.50
A DOLL'S HOUSE, Henrik Ibsen. 80pp. 27062-9 $1.00
HEDDA GABLER, Henrik Ibsen. 80pp. 26469-6 $1.50
GHOSTS, Henrik Ibsen. 64pp. 29852-3 $1.50
VOLPONE, Ben Jonson. 112pp. 28049-7 $1.50
DR. FAUSTUS, Christopher Marlowe. 64pp. 28208-2 $1.00
THE MISANTHROPE, Molière. 64pp. 27065-3 $1.00

PLAYS

THE EMPEROR JONES, Eugene O'Neill. 64pp. 29268-1 $1.50

BEYOND THE HORIZON, Eugene O'Neill. 96pp. 29085-9 $1.50

ANNA CHRISTIE, Eugene O'Neill. 80pp. 29985-6 $1.50

THE LONG VOYAGE HOME AND OTHER PLAYS, Eugene O'Neill. 80pp. 28755-6 $1.00

RIGHT YOU ARE, IF YOU THINK YOU ARE, Luigi Pirandello. 64pp. (Available in U.S. only) 29576-1 $1.50

SIX CHARACTERS IN SEARCH OF AN AUTHOR, Luigi Pirandello. 64pp. (Available in U.S. only) 29992-9 $1.50

HANDS AROUND, Arthur Schnitzler. 64pp. 28724-6 $1.00

ANTONY AND CLEOPATRA, William Shakespeare. 128pp. 40062-X $1.50

HAMLET, William Shakespeare. 128pp. 27278-8 $1.00

HENRY IV, William Shakespeare. 96pp. 29584-2 $1.00

RICHARD III, William Shakespeare. 112pp. 28747-5 $1.00

OTHELLO, William Shakespeare. 112pp. 29097-2 $1.00

JULIUS CAESAR, William Shakespeare. 80pp. 26876-4 $1.00

KING LEAR, William Shakespeare. 112pp. 28058-6 $1.00

MACBETH, William Shakespeare. 96pp. 27802-6 $1.00

THE MERCHANT OF VENICE, William Shakespeare. 96pp. 28492-1 $1.00

A MIDSUMMER NIGHT'S DREAM, William Shakespeare. 80pp. 27067-X $1.00

MUCH ADO ABOUT NOTHING, William Shakespeare. 80pp. 28272-4 $1.00

AS YOU LIKE IT, William Shakespeare. 80pp. 40432-3 $1.50

THE TAMING OF THE SHREW, William Shakespeare. 96pp. 29765-9 $1.00

TWELFTH NIGHT; OR, WHAT YOU WILL, William Shakespeare. 80pp. 29290-8 $1.00

ROMEO AND JULIET, William Shakespeare. 96pp. 27557-4 $1.00

ARMS AND THE MAN, George Bernard Shaw. 80pp. (Available in U.S. only) 26476-9 $1.50

PYGMALION, George Bernard Shaw. 96pp. (Available in U.S. only) 28222-8 $1.00

HEARTBREAK HOUSE, George Bernard Shaw. 128pp. (Available in U.S. only) 29291-6 $1.50

THE SCHOOL FOR SCANDAL, Richard Brinsley Sheridan. 96pp. 26687-7 $1.50

ANTIGONE, Sophocles. 64pp. 27804-2 $1.00

OEDIPUS REX, Sophocles. 64pp. 26877-2 $1.00

ELECTRA, Sophocles. 64pp. 28482-4 $1.00

MISS JULIE, August Strindberg. 64pp. 27281-8 $1.50

THE PLAYBOY OF THE WESTERN WORLD AND RIDERS TO THE SEA, J. M. Synge. 80pp. 27562-0 $1.50

THE IMPORTANCE OF BEING EARNEST, Oscar Wilde. 64pp. 26478-5 $1.00

LADY WINDERMERE'S FAN, Oscar Wilde. 64pp. 40078-6 $1.00

BOXED SETS

FIVE GREAT POETS: Poems by Shakespeare, Keats, Poe, Dickinson and Whitman, Dover. 416pp. 26942-6 $5.00

NINE GREAT ENGLISH POETS: Poems by Shakespeare, Keats, Blake, Coleridge, Wordsworth, Mrs. Browning, FitzGerald, Tennyson and Kipling, Dover. 704pp. 27633-3 $9.00

FIVE GREAT ENGLISH ROMANTIC POETS, Dover. 496pp. 27893-X $5.00

SEVEN GREAT ENGLISH VICTORIAN POETS: Seven Volumes, Dover. 592pp. 40204-5 $7.50

SIX GREAT AMERICAN POETS: Poems by Poe, Dickinson, Whitman, Longfellow, Frost and Millay, Dover. 512pp. (Available in U.S. only) 27425-X $6.00